RAIDERS OF THE LOST R's

Steven Wright

"But when the Son of Man comes in his glory, and all the holy angels with him, then will he sit on the throne of his glory. Before him all the nations will be gathered, and he will separate them one from another, as the shepherd separates the sheep from the goats. He will set the sheep on his right hand, but the goats on the left. Then the King will tell them on his right hand, `Come, blessed of my Father, inherit the kingdom prepared for you from the foundation of the world; for I was hungry, and you gave me food to eat; I was thirsty, and you gave me drink; I was a stranger, and you took me in; naked, and you clothed me; I was sick, and you visited me; I was in prison, and you came to me.`

Matthew 25:31-36 (Wold English Version)

Raiders of the Lost R's was first published in 2007 and is Copyrighted © by Steven Wright, Publisher
7102 Hwy. 41a Pleasant View, TN. 37146

Cover art work Copyright © 2007 by Steven Wright

ISBN 978-0-6151-4736-9
ID 672073

All rights reserved.

No part of this book may be reproduced or transmitted in any form, or by any means, electronic or mechanical, including photocopying or recording, or by any information storage and retrieval system, without permission in writing from the publisher. Any of these actions is strictly prohibited without the expressed written consent of the publisher, Steven Wright.

This book was published in collaboration with God's Wright Way Healing Ministry. For more information you can visit the web site listed. http://www.godhealme.org This book and ministry are dedicated to helping restore the balance to the mind, body, and spirit. God's word is a natural and spiritual part of mans well- being. This book was designed to help reveal some of God's word and purpose for man.

This book is dedicated to my wonderful family who has been a true blessing in my life.

Thank you to Lulu publishing for making this publishing process a dream come true.
www.lulu.com

CONTENTS

ABOUT THE AUTHOR ....…............. 4

INTRODUCTION ....…...…....... 5
    What are the lost R's

CHAPTER 1 ....…..……....... 17
    Respect

CHAPTER 2 ....…..…….….. 34
    Responsibility

CHAPTER 3 ....…..…….….. 47
    Religion

CHAPTER 4 ....…..….................. 60
    Realization

CHAPTER 5 ....….................. 74
    Reflection

POEMS ....…..…............….... 89

BIBLIOGRAPHY ....…............... 91

ABOUT THE AUTHOR

Steve Wright was born and raised in Cincinnati, Ohio where he graduated from High School. He then moved to Nashville, Tennessee to attend David Lipscomb College where he graduated with a Bachelor's Degree in Youth Ministry.

He then spent two years and four months in Yucatán, Mexico on a mission trip. This time was spent serving Mayan Indian natives in remote regions of the Yucatán Peninsula. He moved back to the Unites States in 1990 and settled back in Nashville. He entered the Nashville Metropolitan Police Academy and graduated as a patrol officer in 1993. He then met his wife and moved to Cheatham County. He transferred to the Sheriff's Department where he serves as a patrol deputy.

He is a certified D.A.R.E.® instructor to help kids stay away from drugs and violence. For six years he has taught about 700 sixth graders in four different middle schools while helping to build their confidence and self-esteem by being a positive influence and role model. He is also involved in helping people overcome addictions by using several programs and resources available in the community by utilizing support groups from area churches and volunteers.

Steve has recently received his certification as a Homeopathic Practitioner, Herbal Practitioner, Homeopathic Mental Sciences Practitioner, Nutritional Practitioner, and a Licensed Minister in God's Natural Healing Way Ministries Inc. He uses God's natural healing ways to help people feel better and overcome addictions, traumas, stress, and any other source that can affect the mind, body, and spirit in a negative way. Restoring over all health is Steve's life ministry now. Steve felt compelled and called in his ministry to write this book. He wants to offer his message and experience to as many people as possible. This will help fulfill his dream of sharing how we all can receive God's health and happiness by letting HIM direct us and by serving one another. You can learn more about his efforts by visiting his website: www.godhealme.org. May you be enriched and blessed through God's purpose and design.

RAIDERS OF THE LOST R'S

INTRODUCTION

Imagine if you will an old naval ship like the H.M.S. Victory sailing on the high seas. It has several powerful guns along with an experienced crew ready to defend itself. The captain is noble in word and deed. He and his crew are bound together by loyalty and courage both to each other and to their purpose. Hiding in the dark of night was the most ruthless and cunning pirate known to man, his name was Captain Arduous. His ship and crew were inferior in size and firepower. The element of surprise was his weapon so he took the perfect moment to strike because he knew there was precious cargo to be had. He was ruthless and used every trick in the book to conquer the old naval ship and the noble Captain. He took whatever he wanted and didn't mind killing anyone who stood in his way. It really didn't matter who he hurt or what he destroyed as long as he was rich and in control. The mighty ship lost its noble Captain along with its treasures. The loyal crew fought valiantly to try and stop the pirate, but to no avail. He took both the treasure and the crew to make them his own. He and his Raiders claimed victory.

Does this sound like a story that was just made up? Take another look at it. I used it as a parable in a similar way that Jesus used them to get a point across. In order to understand the parable, I must define the word Raider. Webster's

dictionary defines it as follows: Sudden attacker for desire, gains, or pleasure with ill regard for victims.
Raiders, just like the pirate in the parable, have deliberately attacked our country. They have taken everything they wanted and coerced the people into doing whatever is asked of them. Our mighty country with its noble leader has become virtually powerless to the Raider's tactics They have looted the four R's, which are essential and precious to our country. The four R's consist of: respect, responsibility, religion, and realization. These are the precious treasures the Raiders have taken. This means that anyone who would deliberately attack people or things in order to please their own desires is considered to be a Raider. They do not care who they step on or the method they use to do it. No one is immune to the destruction and injuries inflicted by a Raider. There is no regard for race, gender, social status, or economic level when being attacked by a Raider. I'm sure you have one or more person in mind while I'm describing the actions of a Raider because they have exploited us all. The Raiders I am talking about in our society are very dangerous and must be either stopped or blanketed very soon or we will suffer some fatal consequences. One of history's most successful Raiders was Adolph Hitler. He used every means available to destroy the four R's. One of his most useful tools was the media. The power that he wielded was used to manipulate leaders. Once you control the mind of society, then you can control their actions. The media was a very successful tool he used to help control the minds of society. He said, "All propaganda has to be popular and has to adapt its spiritual level to the perception of the least intelligent of those towards whom it intends to direct itself."
It doesn't matter if you consider him a genius or a lunatic; the point is he was a master at being a Raider of the R's. He realized that by putting his strategy in very simple terms to the people with little education, the media could help him do

just about anything because everyone swallowed his messages hook, line, and sinker.
Some Raiders are in fact murderers. When you have complete control over a society, then your actions have no consequences. No one will oppose you when you use your power to kill, murder, execute, or perform genocide. A Raider can also be a murderer in a figurative way as well. When you use your control, power, and influence to destroy or kill a society, then you are just as guilty. Charles Mansion is a prime example. The question of whether or not he actually killed someone is irrelevant here. The point is that no one can deny his evil ability to control the minds and actions of his followers to the point of murder. The mastermind of a murderous plot is just as guilty as the thugs who complete the plan. Raiders are often times people we are acquainted with and are sometimes close to. Agatha Christie said, "Every murderer is somebody's old friend". How many times have we heard in the news when a murderer is caught and a close friend or relative is being interviewed and we here them say, "I just can't believe this can happen, they would never do anything like this or hurt anyone". Raiders are masters at clouding emotions and reality. They try to get everyone to believe that everything is normal and acceptable. `If you value your freedom then pay close attention to this book so you can do everything in your power to protect life, liberty, and the pursuit of happiness against these Raiders.

With all of these things in mind, I can now expound on the lost R's. Many people think that the three R's are reading, writing, and arithmetic, but not in this case. Those R's will be the topics for a different book in the future. The R's I am talking about are **R**espect, **R**esponsibility, **R**eligion, and **R**ealization. Obviously these R's have been lost because Raiders have attacked them. They have attacked the R's because they are either ignorant of the importance of the R's, or apathetic towards them. They either have chosen not to abide by these R's or have not been taught the significance of them. The lack of responsibility of parents to teach their kids the value of these R's is of utmost importance. Parents must show their children that they not only care about their education, but their lives as well.

When parents are apathetic or clueless to what their children are being taught, then it comes to no surprise when kids are academically lost. They get frustrated, and then act out. This leads to discipline problems, laziness, and the desire to quit trying.

This all stems from the parent's lack of responsibility to help their children learn and develop mental skills by neglecting the time kids need to spend with their parents. What better way to show a child you care and love them than by spending time listening to them and helping them grow during their school years. Kids need a parent's time and attention. A teacher shared this quote with me from Ron Edmonds. Its powerful message is what we must adopt as parents for the sake of our kids education. This was hanging on the teacher's wall.

"We can, whenever and wherever we choose, successfully teach all children whose schooling is of interest to us. We already know more than we need to do that. Whether or not we do it will finally depend on how we feel about the fact that we haven't so far".

It is kind of a shame that parents seem to take action only when the situation is almost out of control or beyond correction. They see what a neglectful job they have established in their kids' lives, then they try to show everyone they care when it is too late. How distressing this is!

The lack of proper role models is also a contributing factor. The effects, however, can be seen and felt now with the ever-increasing crime and murder rates among juveniles. I was very fortunate enough to have several positive role models in my life. Even to this day, I see some of my old friends who surrounded themselves with negative role models. They always say they regret the things they did and wish they would have not listened to negative peer pressure. No matter where you turn, there is a celebrity doing something outrageously immoral or grossly inappropriate. The list is endless with well-known people from TV, radio, movies, music, and sports. At the MTV awards in 2003, a very popular female celebrity leaned over and French kissed two other female stars while performing on stage. During the Super Bowl, two celebrity pop stars were grinding all over each other as part of the half time entertainment when one of them ripped off a part of their costume to expose a bare female breast. This definitely shows a lack of respect, responsibility, and morals. Its no wonder our kids are growing up confused with no sense of ethics. There is almost no one to be a positive role model for them.

 A detailed study and explanation of the R's is very important in order to know how to defend against the attacks of Raiders. We must stand our ground and protect our country and its freedom. The very foundation of our great nation has been based on the principles of these R's. Our founding fathers had in mind a nation that would be established and maintained by these R's when the Declaration of Independence was written. They also realized that the common bond holding society together was the implementation of one nation under God. The strength, prosperity, and success of our country depends on this motto being put into action through faith. God has clearly given instructions to man on how to live in peace and harmony. What better way to establish a nation then by taking these God given R's and making them the building blocks of society.

How does a Raider attack these R's? When they disregard the rights and freedom of society as a whole then it causes a minority rules instead of a majority rules atmosphere. When a single person or a small number of people have control over a large number of people, then it is easy for the minority number to impose their will over the majority. It breeds and promotes a Darwin evolution type atmosphere. This would be a survival of the strongest or dog eat dog world.
How does that promote respect? It doesn't. The moral aspect of this is wrong by its very nature. If a dictatorship is the correct way to govern a society, then only the strong, or wealthy are right. The temptation to be greedy and corrupt is just too great to overcome without the help from the divine creator, God. Unfortunately, this has been the case more times than not throughout history. We can name three times more bad leaders than good ones. That is why we have a popular phrase, "Absolute power corrupts absolutely". It is possible for a ruler to be a righteous person. The bible does have a few examples of some kings in Israel that did follow Gods' laws. When these kings followed Gods' examples of how to treat people, they enjoyed prosperity. Our Creator has endowed us with a purpose and a plan. This is evident when our fore fathers wrote the Declaration of Independence. The very first part of the **Declaration of Independence** clearly shows the pattern for a God based society. Here is what is says:

> When in the course of human events, it becomes necessary for one people to dissolve the political bands which have connected them with another, and to assume among the powers of the earth, Nature's <u>God entitle them</u>, a decent respect to the opinions of mankind requires that they should declare the causes which impel them to the separation. We hold these truths to be self-evident, that all men are created equal, <u>that they are endowed by their Creator with certain unalienable Rights, that among</u>

these are Life, Liberty, and the pursuit of Happiness.

Raiders are against the intent and meaning of our Constitution. They are trying to deny the fact that it affirms a divine Creator with a perfect plan for man and nature. It was written with a religiously moral concept to help govern us all with the help of our Divine Creator. Here is what the beginning of our **Constitution** says:

(PREAMBLE) We the people of the United States, in order to form a more perfect union, establish Justice, insure domestic Tranquility, provide for the common defense, promote the general Welfare, and secure the Blessings of Liberty to ourselves and our Posterity, do ordain and establish this Constitution for the Unites States of America.

Let me explain how we are to go about forming a more perfect union, insuring domestic tranquility, and promote the general welfare of our people. There are several words and phrases that are taken directly from the Creator's instructions for all of mankind. God is love. Love is the perfect binding agent. God's love is what facilitates a more perfect union. *"For I would have you know how greatly I strive for you, and for them at Laodicea, and for as many as have not seen my face in the flesh; that their hearts may be comforted, they **being knit together in love**, and unto all riches of the full assurance of understanding, that they may know the mystery of God, [even] Christ, in whom are all the treasures of wisdom and knowledge hidden".* (Col. 2:1-3) The bible is full of examples of how we are to treat each other as brothers and to take other people into consideration before ourselves. *" A new commandment I give unto you, that ye love one another; even as I have loved you, that ye also love one another".* (John 13:34) This would truly promote the general welfare of our people and society. God has granted us every freedom in Him. Freedom is one of His blessings we enjoy. *"For ye, brethren, were called for freedom; only [use] not your freedom for an occasion to the flesh, but through love be servants one to another"*. (Gal. 5:13) We have all the freedom in the heavens and earth to enjoy spreading love and kindness to everyone in everything we do. This freedom is not to indulge in the selfish desires and lusts of the flesh, but to serve one another in brotherly love. God is the source of all blessings and liberty. He has given us the Spirit to enjoy freedom. *"Now the Lord is that Spirit: and where the Spirit of the Lord is, there is liberty"*. (2 Corinthians 3:17)

I understand that our founding fathers made mistakes and were not perfect. This is why I do not believe in burning people believed to be witches at the steak or the atrocities of slavery. Some were acting in accordance with their religious convictions which may be a noble intention but erroneous in fundamental human ethical philosophy. They did however give us the foundation from which to build a society recognizing God as the ultimate guide and authority. James Madison, the fourth president, known as "The Father of Our Constitution" made the following statement, "We have staked the whole of all our political institutions upon the capacity of mankind for self-government, upon the capacity of each and all of us to govern ourselves, to control ourselves, to sustain ourselves according to the Ten Commandments of God." This pretty much sums up the content and purpose of this book. We need respect, responsibility, and religion to govern, control, and sustain ourselves according to the Ten Commandments, which God has disclosed to us. In order for man to live together in harmony, we must help defend and take care of one another in the same manner we would take care of ourselves. That is the way God wants us to act toward each other. Patrick Henry, a patriot and Founding Father of our country said, "It cannot be emphasized too strongly or too often that this great nation was founded not by religionists but by Christians, not on religions but on the Gospel of Jesus Christ". That is what our country should be… one nation under God. This should not only be our motto, but our conviction as a God fearing nation established by Christians.

When this is attacked and destroyed by Raiders who may be members of our own society, then the fall and decline of society will not be very far behind. This will be illustrated in a later chapter. I did receive an email from a friend of mine about a minister in Kansas that was asked to lead a prayer to open the session of the Senate. This minister said exactly what I am talking about and has the spirit of conviction towards God that we all need to start practicing. Here is the email message, which I received from my friend:

> This is an interesting prayer, which was given in Kansas at the opening session of their Senate. It seems prayer still upsets some people. When Minister Joe Wright was asked to open the new session of the Kansas Senate, everyone was expecting the usual generalities, but this is what they heard:
> "Heavenly Father, we come before you today to ask your forgiveness and to seek your direction and guidance. We know Your Word says, "Woe to those who call evil good," but that is exactly what we have done. We have lost our spiritual equilibrium and reversed our values. We confess that we have ridiculed the absolute truth of Your Word and called it Pluralism. We have exploited the poor and called it the lottery. We have rewarded laziness and called it welfare. We have killed our unborn and called it choice. We have shot abortionists and called it justifiable. We have neglected to discipline our children and called it building self-esteem. We

have abused power and called it politics. We have coveted our neighbor's possessions and called it ambition. We have polluted the air with profanity and pornography and called it freedom of expression. We have ridiculed the time-honored values of our forefathers and called it enlightenment. Search us, Oh, God, and know our hearts today; cleanse us from every sin and set us free. Guide and bless these men and women who have been sent to direct us to the center of Your will and to openly ask these things in the name of Your Son, the living Savior, Jesus Christ. Amen!"
The response was immediate. A number of legislators walked out during the prayer in protest. In 6 short weeks, Central Christian Church, where Rev. Wright is pastor, logged more than 5,000 phone calls with only 47 of those calls responding negatively. The church is now receiving international requests for copies of this prayer from India, Africa, and Korea. Commentator Paul Harvey aired this prayer on his radio program, "The Rest of the Story," and received a larger response to this program than any other aired. With the Lord's help, may this prayer sweep over our nation and wholeheartedly become our desire so that we again can be called "one nation under God."

It is kind of ironic that this minister has the same last name as I do and shares the same spirit of these convictions. I guess that two Wrights don't make it wrong. After all, it took two Wrights to be the first to fly a plane. If only our Senators and nation would adopt the same kind of devotion with a sense of urgency to return to Godly conduct, then maybe God would heal our country and return us to prosperity rather than suffering and despair. Mr. Joe Wright was talking about Raiders in his prayer. The spirit of his supplication is one we all should adopt so that Raiders will realize the damage they have caused, and also the hope they have if they would only return to God and His precepts. You may not agree with some of the political issues involved, but the plea for our leaders and people to return to righteous living should be rooted right away. Will our children ever know what prayer is in a public place? How will God listen if we don't teach them to pray?

It is hard for me to understand exactly why Raiders would really want to tear down a foundation, which gave them a place to stand in the first place. Maybe it is because that history has a way of repeating itself. The children of Israel in the Old Testament had a cycle of events, which provides us with both a model and a warning. Their cycle shows a blatant disregard for the R's after a period of prosperity. God would send a message to Israel warning them not to continue with their disrespectful ways. When the message was ignored, terrible things happened. Israel would then cry to God for forgiveness after suffering for a while. God would hear their cry and deliver them from suffering. Israel would then enjoy a period of prosperity again until the cycle would repeat itself. Sometimes they would be so wicked and perverse that God had to completely destroy every living thing. It is logical to conclude that God is very patient until evilness reaches a severe level. It is then that He must completely destroy it before it continues to spread. God gives man every chance in the world to change from his evil ways before destruction comes. Sometimes mankind listens and is spared from the wrath of God, but sometimes he refuses to listen and he is destroyed because of his own selfish desires. The same example can be shown in prison inmates and their recidivism rates. Sometimes they learn and listen to better themselves to become a productive member of society. When they do not, their cycle of erroneous behavior continues and the punishment keeps getting more severe. When the heinous and immoral deeds reach a certain level, then the death penalty or destruction of life can result.

Our nation has enjoyed a period of prosperity. Raiders have started our nation on the road to terrible things. God has sent several warning messages. It is our choice now to listen to God who has provided our nation with prosperity, or listen to Raiders who care about nothing except the benefit and gain for themselves. I prefer to listen to God by applying all of the R's in my life to be a part of a meaningful society. I am also prepared to strongly defend God's honor and dignity for His followers. We must adopt the attitude of Charles André Joseph Marie de Gaulle when he said, "If I live, I will fight, wherever I must, as long as I must, until the enemy is defeated and the national stain washed clean". God has given us instructions on how to be a righteous and productive nation. We have to preserve His ways. We must fight until the Raiders stain is washed clean even if it costs us our lives.

CHAPTER 1
RESPECT

The very clever pirate, Arduou, now has many subjects to control. He realizes that brute force is only temporary so he immediately begins scheming on how to get them to comply willingly. He quickly fills them with promises of happiness and wealth if they would only accept him as leader. He throws his stolen treasures around to them like a master throws scraps to a dog. He takes them on exciting and dangerous adventures. Soon they begin to emulate the same characteristics as Arduou. They not only have accepted his leadership, but also have become excellent backstabbing, cut- throat, and vicious people. If any member of the crew becomes slow or inefficient, they simply get rid of them. They circle victims like vultures ready to satisfy only their personal lusts and greed. As long as their lusts are satisfied, they are loyal. The loyalty grows stronger with each plunder of self-gratification. They now take pleasure in being a Raider. Loyalty belongs to lust now. Their own gratification has become their god.

I can't help thinking about a song from the Queen of soul, Aretha Franklin, when I hear the word RESPECT. This song has spanned several generations to clearly become a true classic. I am grateful she has caused the spelling of the word to stick in our minds. My wish is that the meaning would stick in our minds as well. Webster's defines respect as: "esteem, honor, consideration, hold in honor". There is a certain power generated from this word that Aretha realized and obviously tapped into. I feel the reason this word is so important and powerful is because it compliments the scope of the Golden Rule: "Do unto others as you would have them do unto you". If everyone would show proper respect towards each other, then our society would have strong roots for generations to come. Wouldn't it be great if everyone respected each other?

Respect must be demonstrated as well as taught. Parents need to show kids what respect is by applying it to their lives. I feel that society is losing respect because it is no longer being displayed or taught like it has been in the past. Society has lost its ability to train young men and women to be courteous, respectful, and polite. Things like opening doors for ladies, giving up a seat for a lady, letting an elderly lady or woman with child go ahead in a line, not using profane language in public, or simply saying Sir or Ma'am when talking to an adult. When I am out in public it disturbs me to see young men not opening a door for a woman, or not making way for the elderly or handicapped, and just being downright rude. Rarely do I see people pulling over to make way for a funeral procession. When I attend a sporting event, there is always a disturbing number of people not placing their hands over their hearts or removing hats when the National Anthem is played. I remember being handicapped for about 2 years because of three different surgeries on my arm. Every time I would go out into public I would see people parking in handicapped spaces who were not handicapped. It really makes me upset to see handicapped people being inconvenienced and ignored by physically normal people who are inconsiderate and rude. I now have absolutely no reservations about writing an expensive ticket for someone illegally parked in a handicap spot. I show no mercy and don't want to hear any excuses for this behavior. I believe that laziness is an obvious characteristic of disrespect not only for you, but for others as well. Parking in a handicapped space when you are not supposed to is a true action of laziness and disrespect.

It really makes me sick to see the same, if not worse, attitudes from young ladies. Young people seem to have lost the social graces that used to be the courteous and polite things to do. An example of this is a man asking a girl's father for her hand in marriage. Amy Vanderbilt comments on the same thing by saying, "The reason for this is a practical one. A girl's parents, especially if they have been supporting their daughter, have the right to know just how her fiancée proposes to take care of her after the marriage, in short, what his income is and his savings, if any, and what may be his future expectations." It is sad to say that I rarely find people who actually demonstrate these respectful characteristics. Where has the respect gone?

Once again, Raiders have attacked us. The word respect has little meaning now because of the damage caused by these Raiders. Respect is quickly being lost. I remember watching Rodney Dangerfield telling everyone that he gets no respect. Even though he used humor, the principle is the same. Society has lost respect for many things that were at one time cherished by both young and old. This has caused a cancerous decay in our nation. Martin Luther King Jr. recognized this fact when he said, "Nothing is more dangerous than sincere ignorance and conscientious stupidity". It is truly dangerous when our kids no longer have proper respect. When we claim not to know any better, or simply choose to not care is when we are indeed dangerous. If we choose to be disrespectful then we are very dangerous because we have made ourselves to be our own god. When humans make themselves to be their own god, then anything goes and only the strong survive. The violent take what they want by force. This reminds me of a story I want to share that clearly demonstrates this attitude.

I remember pulling over a 1985 Oldsmobile vehicle with two doors and a soft top around 2:30 a.m. on the West side of town in Nashville. I noticed that there were two occupants and they appeared to be young subjects. Another officer was fairly close to the area and decided to join me. When we approached the vehicle we both saw the butt of a handgun wedged between the driver and passenger seats. We immediately drew our weapons and shouted for the two young males to put their hands on the dashboard where we could see them. For some reason, the driver slowly started reaching towards the seat and I screamed several times, "Hands Up". I took aim at his chest and started squeezing the trigger when he suddenly decided to put his hands up and look at me. We quickly got both subjects out of the car and cuffed them on the ground. Come to find out that the gun was actually a B.B. pistol. I told the young man how close he came to being shot and he answered me by just saying, "So". I asked him if he cared what kind of trouble he put his passenger friend in and his response to me was, "I don't give a f---". The driver was only 17 years old, and the passenger was 18. They admitted to sneaking out of their house and were going to use the gun to scare another kid (17) into paying back some money he owed them. This is the most dangerous kind of behavior when the knowledge of right and wrong are recognized but are deliberately ignored and discarded. They knew that they could have been shot for their actions, but could care less about the consequences. They made themselves to be their own god. I don't identify with their attitude and reasoning. They simply didn't care. Let me share another example. A female called stating that her husband had assaulted her and kicked her out of the house. The husband had already left the scene to go to work by the time she walked down the street to use the phone to call the police. When I arrived the severity of the situation became clear. She is sixteen years old yet legally married to a twenty year old male, and eight and a half months pregnant. They had gotten into an argument when he got angry and hit her several times in the head with his fist. He then shoved her very hard over the coffee table causing her to land on the table, roll over to the edge of the couch, and on the floor. He then picked her back up and kicked her butt (literally) forcing her out the front door telling her not to come back. She landed on the ground falling down the front steps. They do not have a phone in the house so she started walking to her mom's house. She walked about two miles barefooted in 96 degree heat while injured. Remember she is less than two weeks from giving birth. I immediately called for an ambulance to transport her to the ER for an evaluation of the baby. I was stunned when she told me that she did not want to go to the hospital. I tried to get her mom to talk her into it, but they both refused. I tried to get them to think about the safety of the baby but they still would not listen. I sadly finished my report and took out warrants on the father that had done this to her. I asked him later why he didn't take her to the hospital for the baby's sake. He said he didn't care because he wasn't even sure if the baby was his. You can't imagine the swarm of emotions that were going on inside me at this time. It is one thing to not have any respect for yourselves or each other, but it is another thing not to have any respect for an innocent and defenseless baby no matter who the parents may be. Is this what we will become?

Raiders are responsible for the lack of respect for things like, authority, the elderly, patriotism, ethics, and morals. If we really want to become one nation under God, then we must take seriously His words in 1 Peter 2:17 "Show respect for everyone. Love the brotherhood, Fear God. Show respect for the King". Our Declaration of Independence acknowledges the fact that God has given us the right to respect others. This is why our nation was formed to respect the life, liberty, and the pursuit of happiness for everyone. Raiders have attacked respect, but we can use Gods' power to train our society to be respectful again. An ignorant and apathetic society is truly a dangerous society, a society that will eventually destroy itself.

The first part of respect I would like to introduce is towards authority. One of the favorite things for Raiders to do is slander and malign people in position of authority. I have over twelve years of experience as a police officer and believe me; Raiders are hard to deal with when there is a total lack of respect for authority. Talking bad about our President, a teacher, police, parents, or politicians is a Raiders mode of operation. I understand that everyone is entitled to an opinion about these things, but that's not what I am talking about. I am referring to the vicious and unnecessary words about the person. I feel it is all right to disagree about a certain action, decision, or deed a person does, but inappropriate to judge or condemn a person.
The best example is the purpose of this book. I can disagree with all the bad things a Raider does and voice my opinions, but it would be wrong to name a specific Raider in a very high position just to use many descriptive adjectives my mother told me never to use. If I really desire to follow the instructions God has established, then I must respect authority. What better advice and example could I have then one from the ultimate authority himself? This is stated in the book of Romans as follows:

> **Romans 13:1-7 (NLT)** "Obey the government, for God is the one who put it there. All governments have been placed in power by God. So those who refuse to obey the laws of the land are refusing to obey God, and punishment will follow. For the authorities do not frighten people who are doing right, but they frighten those who do wrong. So do what they say, and you will get along well. The authorities are sent by God to help you. But if you are doing something wrong, of course you should

be afraid, for you will be punished. The authorities are established by God for that very purpose, to punish those who do wrong. So you must obey the government for two reasons: to keep from being punished and to keep a clear conscience. Pay your taxes too, for these same reasons. For government workers need to be paid so they can keep on doing the work God intended them to do. Give to everyone what you owe them: Pay your taxes and import duties, and give respect and honor to all whom it is due".

One of the key words is in verse 5 when it mentions the word conscience. We should do the right thing and be respectful towards those who have authority over us because the Spirit of God should guide our conscience. It is difficult to practice the part in verse 3 that says if we want to be free from the one in authority then we should do what is right. The normal response is to gripe, complain, and criticize all the time rather than do the right thing or be part of a solution. I remember working with some officers that were very unhappy with their supervisor. All they did was sit around and complain about the situation and talk bad about the supervisor. The day came when the supervisor left. A new boss came in and fired, demoted, and shuffled around the ones that kept complaining about the old boss. They were not part of the solution, so they were treated as part of the problem.

I feel the overall principle of these verses is for us to be examples to those in authority. If we obey the laws they give to us and always strive to do what is right even though they are doing wrong, then our Christian example will be a light for them to see. Once they have a clear vision of what is right, then it is possible for them to realize the error of their ways and make the proper adjustments to change. Our attitudes and actions should be above reproach. This is when

we can truly be honored and respected. It is in this position we can bestow honor and respect to those who deserve it as is stated in verse 7.
What good would it be for someone to give honor or respect to an authority figure if they themselves were not honorable? My father used to say to me when I was a small boy, "If you want someone to respect and listen to you, then tell them with your actions". This is the best example I could impart. He obviously had authority over me. I always tried to do what he asked of me even though sometimes I would get mad and not like at all whatever it was he was asking me to do. I am ashamed to say that I was rebellious sometimes. This is what Romans is saying **not** to do. I needed to respect his authority more than I did.
It took me a long time to finally realize the principle of Romans 13:1-7. I found that if I was respectful and polite to my father when he was telling me to do something I didn't like, things not only went smoother, but I usually got more in return later. This means that if there is someone in a position of authority telling me what to do, and I don't like it or agree with it, then God is telling me to be respectful and polite. This seems to be very difficult for people to do these days because the skill of being respectful has been lost. This is why it says in Proverbs 15:1, "A gentle answer turns away wrath, but harsh words stir up anger". I have seen this in action several times. As a police officer for several years, I realized that if someone is kind and respectful to me even though they didn't agree with why they were being arrested, then I would be more inclined to help them as much as I could and be a little more lenient. I remember transporting a prisoner from Philadelphia who was accused of homicide. On the way he was well mannered and respectful towards me, so I stopped and got him really good food he had been missing for a long time. He thanked me for not being one of those typical cops with an attitude that give him a hard time

just because of what he did. I thanked him for being respectful to me. I was one of the few he trusted.
Just because I didn't like an action he was being accuse of didn't mean it was acceptable for me to not like him as a person. We were both polite and respectful to each other even under these awkward and unpleasant circumstances. This is the point of being respectful.
Proverbs 15:18 says," A hothead starts fights; a cool-tempered person tries to stop them". Raiders have caused the lack of respect towards authority to spread like cancer almost to the point where it cannot be cured. If we continue to ignore the problem, we will have fatal results. If we are not part of the solution, then we are part of the destructive problem.

The second facet of respect is towards the elderly. This is a very large topic. There have been demonstrations and debates on this subject going on for quite some time now. It is tragic that Raiders have cast respect for the elderly aside like an empty beer bottle. Senior citizens have so much to offer our society if we would only take the time to sit and listen. Raiders are so self absorbed that they do not have anything to offer to the elderly. I feel we should be giving back a whole lot to the elderly because of respect and the fact that we wouldn't enjoy the things we do if they had not sacrificed for us. The attitude of Sir Winston Churchill should apply towards the elderly when he said, "We make a living by what we get; we make a life by what we give". We truly should make a life of giving respect and honor to our Senior citizens.

If we want to follow Gods example, then we should read this: LEVITICUS 19:32, "Show your fear of God by standing up in the presence of elderly and showing respect for the aged. I am the Lord. " It is pretty clear that we should respect the elderly and treat them with dignity and honor for what they have done for us. Raiders want to repay the elderly by not providing funds for medical insurance, prescriptions, social security, and other helpful programs. A large number of Senior citizens are on a very limited income and can't afford these things. Social Security helps them hang on by a thread, but isn't enough in so many cases. Government assistance programs are not much help either. Placing the elderly in nursing homes can be an atrocity. This country is full of lawsuits regarding improper medical care and neglect for the elderly. I don't understand how we can let our own families and friends be treated this way. I could list all day long the reasons why these mistreatments should never occur, but I don't want to beat a dead horse. For the sake of brevity I will only point out this certain principle. We need to take better care of our elderly. If a Senior citizen is on a small budget and is placed in a nursing home which insurance doesn't cover, then something is wrong. The insurance companies keep refusing all kinds of medical treatment that is essential for survival. The prices for medical care are just outrageous for the elderly.

When my mother retired, her monthly payment for medical insurance was just as much as my house payment. This is not right for someone who has worked hard all of their life, retires, and then can't afford medical insurance. This might explain why you see so many places hiring people who are retired. They know they need the extra money to pay for insurance and other related expenses. The word retired has almost become a farce. You have to work again when you quit working. What kind of reward is that for our elderly?

A nice gesture would be to just spend time with the elderly. I feel one of the greatest treasures we can give to someone is our time. Show someone you care just by being there. I understand now that my Grandma didn't really care what presents she got for Christmas. The important thing was that we were all together for Christmas Day spending time with each other. I think that spending time with the elderly shows an immense amount of respect. How much do we respect them?

It would not be fair to just say that Raiders are disrespectful to our elderly without trying to offer some sort of solution. If I am not part of the solution, then I am part of the problem just like the Raiders. One suggestion is to get better acquainted with the elderly and find out what their needs are according to their desires, not ours. A second suggestion is to unite religious organizations to assist not only with personnel, but also with funds for the elderly. Churches could work together and form medical facilities for the elderly just as they have formed places for needy children and foster homes. A third suggestion is to take the list of needs from the elderly and submit it to your local legislatures with a bunch of people's names on it that are registered voters. We still need to voice the truth to the ones that are sworn to represent the people that have elected them. Our legislatures cannot help us if we do not communicate with them about what our needs are. Sometimes the legislators can't relate to the retirement problem because we have not shared with them our concerns about this subject. The point is we need to put love into action towards the elderly. Raiders don't care. Do we?

The third position of respect is toward Patriotism. Raiders have all but destroyed our sense of patriotism. I feel the best definition is from our former President Calvin Coolidge when he said, "Patriotism is easy to understand in America. It means looking out for yourself by looking out for your country." How simplistic yet full of substance this quote is. I feel it is very important to cherish and feel a deep sense of patriotism because it is part of the freedom we fight for. Without it a nation would either be destroyed or destroy itself. I was reading some material by Don Nardo regarding the decline and fall of the Roman Empire and found his insight to be most helpful. He said, "As the Empire slowly grew more and more corrupt, the people's sense of patriotism diminished."

He recognized the fact that when Raiders attack a nation's patriotism, it will decline. There are different aspects of patriotism, which a Raider can attack. Apathy towards our soldiers, veterans, country, freedom, and symbols of our nation's greatness is the venom spread by Raiders. Symbols of our nation's greatness include things like: the American flag, The Pledge of Allegiance, The Star Spangled Banner, and America's Creed.

I will start with apathy towards our soldiers. You would think that we should have learned our lesson during the Korean and Vietnam wars. A large number of Raiders protested and hated our soldiers for doing what they were ordered to do. So many restrictions were placed on them, and because of this, it was difficult to effectively carry out those orders. Whether or not you agree with the reasons for fighting these wars is not the point here. My point is this. If our President decides to send troops somewhere to fight and we do not agree with his reasons for doing so, then we should voice our objection towards the White House and **NOT** to the soldiers performing their duties. The lack of respect towards our soldiers and veterans is one of the greatest disservices we could ever do to our country. I feel it is very wrong to take out political frustrations on our soldiers. Should we send troops to Korea, Vietnam, Afghanistan, Iraq, and Iran is a question that can be debated for years. It doesn't matter whether or not you agree if we should have fought the Spanish American War, Vietnam War, or Terrorist War, our soldiers need to be recognized and appreciated for sacrificing themselves for our country. Should we honor and thank the soldiers that have fought there? Definitely, **YES!** If it weren't for our soldiers, then we would not have the freedoms we enjoy today. Abraham Lincoln recognized this important respect for our soldiers

and their families. Fighting for our freedom and independence made him aware of the enormous respect towards our nation's warriors. The respect from Abraham Lincoln is as follows:
"On that first American Independence Day a band of brave men pledged their lives, their fortunes, and their sacred honor to do the battle for human freedom. With malice toward none, with charity for all, with firmness in the right as God gives us to see the right, let us strive on to finish the work we are in, to bind up the nation's wounds, to care for him who shall have borne the battle and for his widow and orphans, to do all which may achieve and cherish a just and lasting peace among ourselves and with all nations".

What a great model of attitude and importance designed for our country. Respect and gratitude should be the heart of our nation. This falls right in line with what God would have us do. We should listen to God's instructions and be respectful towards each other, especially our veterans. I was very proud when my 9-year-old daughter came home from school one day and recited the American's Creed completely from memory. She attends a private school and is allowed to study the fundamental relationship between God's instructions for mankind, and the respect due to one another. I hope and pray that these words will stay with her forever. It really does refresh my soul to see a fine example of a young lady memorizing such words of respect and wisdom. Here is what she presented to me by memory in 2003:

> "I believe in the United States of America as a Government of the people, by the people, and for the people; whose just powers are derived from the consent of the governed; a democracy in a republic; a sovereign nation of many sovereign states; a perfect union, one and inseparable; established upon these

principles of freedom, equality, and justice,
and humanity for which American patriots
sacrificed their lives and fortunes. I therefore
believe it is my duty to my country to love it,
to support its Constitution, to obey its laws; to
respect its flag, and to defend it against all
enemies". (William Tyler Page)

This naturally leads me to lack of respect towards patriotism in our public school systems. We are supposed to be learning about what our country stands for, and what it is based upon as well. How can kids be taught the fundamental truths that God has established for all of humanity when you can't even mention His name without offending someone? Our reason for our existence was based on the principle of being one nation under God. The whole purpose for the Pledge of Allegiance is to remind us that we need to respect God's guidelines so that we can be thankful for liberty and justice for all. This is what will keep our nation together and strong, being bound to each other under God's instruction. If there is any child or adult who does not want to recite the Pledge of Allegiance, that is fine as long as they respect the right of those who do. I feel they should be able to adequately explain why they refuse to do so. I also feel that this needs to be done in the presence of several veterans who are handicapped because of war injuries. Then explain why to the widows and children who no longer have a father. Most importantly, they need to explain why they refuse to say the words one nation under God to the Almighty Himself on judgment day when every knee shall bow and every tongue confess that Jesus Christ is Lord. We must realize that our flag, national anthem, pledge of allegiance, creed, and seal are just symbols to help remind us of the sacrifices made to be a free country. They must be taught and preserved with the acknowledgment and respect given to the Supreme guardian of truth. What are we teaching our kids in school isn't really the question we should be asking. We should be more worried about what we are NOT teaching our kids in school.

The fifth phase of respect I want to point out is towards ethics and morality. A more specific and detailed explanation of these words is spelled out in a later chapter, so I will briefly describe them. When I mention morals and ethics together, I am talking about the ability to stand firm on convictions of what is right and wrong. Raiders have successfully torn down our ability to stand up for what is right, just, or good. This is a blatant lack of respect for ethics and morals itself. Our movies and T.V. shows used to be filled with wonderful actors who would fight to the death for a just cause. The good guys were always defending honor, dignity, and integrity. These characteristics displayed true morals and ethics that children loved to imitate. It was every boys dream to be just like Gene Autrey, The Lone Ranger, Roy Rogers, Sheriff Andy Taylor, and even Zorro. One of my favorites was Superman because he stood for truth, justice, and the American way. These are all fine examples of positive role models. Parents were refreshed to see their kids acting like these characters because they realized that these stories had ethics. It is sad to say that it is difficult to name any actors or actresses who are good examples of positive peer pressure and acceptable role models. Kids are just not being taught good morals and ethics anymore. This also causes a lack of respect towards these things because they fail to see the importance of them. People have no respect for being engaged or married. Amy Vanderbilt said, "Engagements were made to be broken. Never, if you have just become engaged, assume that the engagement will necessarily terminate in marriage. If more engagements were honestly viewed before marriages are entered into there would be far fewer divorces." She realized the importance of taking a relationship seriously in the beginning so that if it does result in marriage, it will last. This will show respect for each other and for the ideology for marriage itself.

I remember listening to my mother read from all kinds of books with positive messages and stories. Fables were excellent examples of literature that teach us morals. Fables are stories that have animals with human actions and characteristics. Their various experiences help teach us about life, and the way human beings behave. Aesop's fables are probably considered the most common and popular. They have been in existence for over 2,500 years. Part of the reason for their success is because of their purpose. Using a basic code of morality or fundamental truth is a very ingenious method of teaching. That is why it has stood the test of time and transcended various cultures. Another example of this principle is in India. Jakatas are stories about Buddha and his experiences as different animals. These also teach different morals. The point is that parents used to take time and read to children. The material had a purpose and meaning. Reading about good morals and ethics to children is what life is all about. The respect of this heart-warming privilege has almost been lost.

Raiders are trying their best to put a stop to this action so that their own agenda will be taught instead. They show a complete lack of respect towards instilling morals and ethics into the minds of our children. I wish that these Raiders would adopt the principle of the Masonic code of Etiquette and Conduct. It says, "If you live according to the teachings of masonry, if you make yourself known to the world as a mason; if your conduct is above reproach, then the people in the community will appreciate and respect free masonry". If we would teach our kids the importance of good morals and ethics in our own lives then maybe our society could respect true convictions of what is positive, healthy, and good. We would then become proper role models for our kids. This is why we need to respect morals and ethics. I could write several books on the topic of respect alone, but for now I must move on to explain other things as well.

Let us unite together against the Raiders under the banner of RESPECT. The power to overcome is from God. We must respect Him and His ways in order to properly show respect towards each other. The whole duty of man is summed up in this statement, "Love the Lord your God with everything, then love your neighbor as you would yourself". Let's put God first so He can direct our path. If we would put this into practice, then our respect for His authority, the elderly, patriotism, and His code of morals can make our world a better place to live with purpose and guidance. Why wouldn't we want a society and nation based on respect and directed by God?

CHAPTER 2
RESPONSIBILITY

The price of greatness is responsibility. - Sir Winston Churchill

Pirate Arduou has successfully recruited and trained a new generation of Raiders. They are blood -thirsty barbarians who answer to no one except their own wants. They take what they want, when they want it and whoa be to whoever tries to stand in their way. There are no repercussions for what they do because they live by no one's law but their own. How are they going to be held accountable if there is no one to enforce laws or object to their actions? Raiders enjoy the lawless life without discipline or responsibility. This only makes them deadlier than before. Captain Arduou is a master of evil motivation and manipulation.

Our nation is indeed considered to be a great one because of the rewards through responsibilities our leaders and warriors have achieved. A part of this was discussed in the previous chapter when I gave all the credit and praise to our veterans for their sacrifices through duty and responsibility. One example of meeting responsibility head on against all odds was the leadership ability of General George Patton. Here is a quote about the aspect of fear and the responsibility of duty of General Patton. "From his own personal experiences in action he knew something of the nature of fear and recognized the fact that its basis is awareness of danger. This he regarded as healthy…. This lead him to examine the factors which in the past had enabled men in battle to fight fear with courage, to advance or stand firm and not bolt in panic". – H. Essamé

Yes, Raiders have attacked our sense of responsibility. Let me first define the word, and then it will be revealed exactly how Raiders have all but negated responsibility. Webster's defines the word responsibility as: state of being responsible, obligation. It defines responsible as: accountable, reliable, distinguishing between right and wrong.

It is kind of obvious that the word responsibility conveys several implications. When using the word responsibility, the concept of accountability is at the core of the meaning. Raiders have done an excellent job of massacring our nation's obligation to responsible behavior. It seems like no one is held accountable for anything that is said or done anymore. When accountability has been lost then a lawless society takes over. This is the breeding ground for chaos, rebellion, civil war, and the birth of dictators. This leads us to another sense of the word, consequences. It must be a natural part of responsibility. I have taught kids for years the D.A.R.E. definition of the word. In short, it is, the things that happen because of something you do, or choose not to do. Once again, Raiders have been hard at work by taking away the consequences of our actions. This is why you hear the phrase; it's not my fault. Blaming others for what we have done ourselves is the perfect example of the damage caused by Raiders. There is no responsibility when there are no consequences for our actions and words. Our society wonders why juveniles are committing so many dangerous and serious crimes. It is because there are no stern consequences for their behavior. Responsibility also carries with it the idea of discipline. This means that there are no rules or standards to adhere to. Juvenile delinquents have little regard for responsibilities, consequences, or discipline. You can say the same about some adults too.

Raiders have made sure that discipline has been subdued. Self-gratification is the only motivation for action. Without discipline, there is chaos and madness. It is most difficult to choose the right thing to do when there is no discipline of self-control to start with. You can't control the outcome of your situation when you can't control yourself first. This is why the concept of humility and thinking of other people before yourself is repeated throughout the bible. God wants mankind to be responsible to Him and towards each other. When mankind starts to turn away from God by becoming a Raider that is when the fall of man begins. Adam was kicked out of the Garden of Eden because he felt he was not responsible for his actions. This is why he blamed it all on Eve. He definitely did not keep in mind the consequences of his actions when he made the choice to eat of the forbidden fruit. Both Adam and Eve lacked the discipline to keep God's decrees when they faced the ultimate Raider, the Devil serpent himself. God said in Job 36:10-12 (KJV) "He openeth also their ear to discipline, and commandeth that they return from iniquity. If they obey and serve Him, they shall spend their days in prosperity, and their years in pleasure. But if they obey not, they shall perish by the sword, and they shall die without knowledge." Raiders might be fooling themselves right now, but eventually they will be held accountable or responsible for what they have done. This is shown in Romans 14:12 (KJV) "So then every one of us shall give account of himself to God." I prefer to stand before the Almighty God representing loyalty to Him by my life's example of responsible actions and discipline. I hope this book inspires you to do the same.

First, I would like to expound on the word accountability as it relates to responsibility. I prefer to think of it as giving a response or report for actions. We all have to give an account for something to someone in our lives. Examples of this are: taxes, job performance, relationships, judges, etc.

Somewhere there is someone in a position of higher authority that we must explain our actions to. Most religions will agree that we will all give an account for what we have done to a Supreme Being, God, once we have passed from this earth.

My point is that in order to maintain structure and stability we must be able to report to someone in authority to make sure our actions are correct. If you become the ultimate authority then who will make sure your decisions are good ones? Who is there to report to? You are able to do good or bad with power. This is a very important point to remember. We have several examples from history that can demonstrate this point. Hitler and Mussolini had their way with society because they had become the ultimate authority. They were not being held accountable to anyone for their actions. When in this position, they used all kinds methods and techniques to do whatever they wanted. Deciding to intimidate, force, and coerce helped further complete their plans. They made it sound all good and proper to win over the minds and hearts of the public. This is what John Weiss says about it in his book, "It is true, of course, that Nazi propagandists liked to present their movement as the direct heir of a Frederick the Great, a Bismarck, or a Nietzsche, but this could be done only by arbitrary selection, simple distortion, or outright falsehood." They told the people what they wanted to hear by promising them the moon. It didn't matter if it was the truth or not. Then they would give them something to believe in and die for just like mindless slaves. The actions of the people go unquestioned because it is the will of the leader. There is no accountability for the loss of lives or lands. Self-gratification rules the ruler, and therefore rules the people. The people don't seem to mind because they believe in their cause.

 This destructive behavior is not only tolerable, but also accepted. St. Augustine tasted the flavor of not being accountable for his actions. He wrote in his confessions that when he was allowed to do whatever he pleased, he was not accountable to anyone. He then seized the opportunity to indulge in self-gratification. He said he lost himself in a multitude of things. He even lusted in his youth, to be satiated in things below; and he dared to grow wild again, with his various and shadowy desires: his beauty consumed away, and he stank in the eyes of the Lord; pleasing himself, and desiring to please and gain favor in the eyes of men.

This seems to prove without a doubt, that without accountability in self-gratification, destruction is near. God has repeated this message for thousands of years. If we would listen to God rather than to our own lusts and desires, then we would experience the true purpose and meaning of life.
The whole purpose of life should be to please God and to help one another. How many times did He warn Israel to turn from self-gratification and live like God had shown them to live? Way too many! God would send a messenger to warn them to return to righteous living so they could straighten up. If they did not listen, terrible things and destruction followed. This is a natural cycle of events. St. Augustine did experience a combination of emotions and events, which he describes in his confessions. He remembers one of the things that bothered him the most was acceptance and praise he received from his friends for doing things without being held accountable for his actions. He confesses that he pursued his desires so stubbornly that shame was no where to be found. The more his friends boasted about his escapades, the more he took pleasure in them. He not only took pleasure in the deeds but in the praise as well. What is worthy of dispraise but vice? How many of us can confess the same kind of sentiments about some of our actions?

Once he came to his senses he realized what the end results of his actions truly were. It became quite clear that it was wretched in the eyes of God. He was indeed accountable to his Creator as well as to his own conscience. Sometimes the mighty fall when the wheels of justice roll their direction and it is then that accountability is stirred. Adam and Eve, Moses, St. Paul, St. Augustine, Napoleon, Hitler, Saddam Hussein, and even companies like Enron were all introduced to accountability through their actions. The virtue of being responsible must incorporate accountability as a proper work ethic; for the quality of the end product depends on it. We should take pride in our work and the way we live. This point is also proven by a well know author, Dr. James Dobson, in his book entitled, "Raising up boys". Most of the people I know who have read his material say that it has helped them immensely. Dr. Dobson uses the work of Robert D. Putnam to make some important illustrations from his book, "Bowling alone, the collapse and revival of American Community". Robert D. Putnam's makes this point on pages 100-101:

>He interviewed nearly 500,000 people over the past 25 years and concluded that we arc increasingly distancing ourselves from each other. The very fabric of our social connections has plummeted, impoverishing our lives and communities. We know our neighbors less, socialize with friends less often, and even grow distant from our families. We belong to fewer organizations that actually meet, such as the Jaycees, Shriners, Elks, and other service clubs. Putnam says that the most significant factor behind the growing isolation is the increase in the number of two-carcer families, thus distancing men and women from their traditional social networks. There is simply no time for much of anything but work and maintaining a household. Television, the Internet, and other forms of

electronic communication have also weakened the linkage between generations and interfered with the transmission of family traditions. In short, Putnam says that the "social capital" of America is shrinking, resulting in more divisiveness and a general breakdown of mutual trust. Parents in the United States spend less time with their children than those in almost any other nation in the world. The result: No one is at home to meet the needs of lonely preschoolers and latchkey children. Dr. Nicholi stressed the undeniable connection between the interruption of parent-child relationships and the escalation of psychiatric problems that we are now seeing. "And if the trend continues," he said, "serious national health problems are inevitable." 95% of all hospital beds in the United States will be occupied by psychiatric patients if the incidence of divorce, child abuse, child molestation, and child neglect continues to soar.

Our nation has neglected its responsibility to family, friends, country, and most importantly, God. The result is a natural decay and breakdown in our social structure. An example of this is the lost responsibility of asking a girl's father for her hand in marriage before the proposal is made to the girl. Amy Vanderbilt's book of Etiquette has this to say about the responsibility of a young man to ask the father of the girl permission for marriage, "The reason for this is a practical one. A girl's parents, especially if they have been supporting their daughter, have the right to know just how her fiancée proposes to take care of her after the marriage, in short, what his income is and his savings, if any, and what may be his future expectations." (p. 117)

Raiders have almost made sure that this polite and respectful social grace has been buried with other lost treasures. This breeds a society of selfish, greedy, and insensitive people.

Not only does it produce a society that is full of unpleasant people, but also a society that is doomed to fail. A million books written on the subject of the importance of accepting, and practicing responsibility would not be enough in order to emphasize the negative results which can occur without proper responsibility. This is why Jesus teaches us the same concept in Luke 6:45, (NLT) "A good person produces good deeds from a good heart, and an evil person produces evil deeds from an evil heart. Whatever is in your heart determines what you say."

What would be the sense of exploring responsibility and accountability without realizing the consequences of each one? Let's define consequences as the outcome of what you choose to do or not to do. Continuing the thoughts from accountability, I will once again use some examples from World War II to introduce the correlation in the company of consequences. Jim Weiss states, "For the regimes of Musolini and Hitler, however, the conquest and permanent exploitation of subject peoples was an unavoidable consequence of their rejection of domestic reform. And even here it may be said that the revolutionary right radically intensified and pushed to extremes those existing and predominant conservative values which did stress the virtues of a warlike culture: authoritarianism, discipline, unity, disdain for dissent, and disregard for the well-being of the masses." Here we have the consequences of several actions and choices.

These leaders made political, economic, and social choices that produced consequences, which affected the entire world. If I were to make a list of these choices it would be an entire volume of books. Even when they chose not to do something, it had an impact on many lives and countries. If you are not responsible enough to be accountable for your choices then you must feel apathetic of the consequences.

This is the foundation of a very humanistic avenue. The problem with this is that it puts a human on the same level or higher as the Creator. God definitely does not tolerate this. He absolutely hates it. This violates the first commandment from the Ten Commandments, which is: Thou shall have no other Gods before me (Exodus 20:3). There are many examples in the bible showing where God despises a humanistic attitude elevated above Him. The consequences were severe and included destruction, diseases, and death. Some scholars believe that Satan was cast out of heaven because he put himself on a level similar or higher than God. His consequences are pretty severe. I feel we need to take this very seriously if we want to be in favor with God and to be pleasing in His sight. I certainly do not want to make the same mistake and suffer the consequence of death or destruction.

Many actions that are in contrast with God's laws have unpleasant consequences. Jim George makes this point when he says, "The sordid example from King David's life teaches us what to beware of- idleness, wrongful sensuousness, and dishonoring the Lord." He recognizes the relationship between responsibility to Gods plan and the consequences that follow if you do them or not. It is always easier to choose the right thing in the eyes of God when you keep in mind the consequences of your choice. Let's be straightforward here. When man relies upon himself for direction, the result is self-destruction. Too often it turns into lawless behavior. I feel we are failing to teach younger generations the principle of consequences. There is a clear example of this in the book of Hosea where the Priests were not teaching the people the correct way of God and the severe consequences of disobeying His laws. If we neglect our responsibility of teaching discipline and instruction to our children then we will summon the same wrath of God upon us. Here is what God says.

"Hear the word of the LORD, O people of Israel! The LORD has filed a lawsuit against you, saying: "There is no faithfulness, no kindness, no knowledge of God in your land. 2 You curse and lie and kill and steal and commit adultery. There is violence everywhere, with one murder after another. 3 That is why your land is not producing. It is filled with sadness, and all living things are becoming sick and dying. Even the animals, birds, and fish have begun to disappear.4 "Don't point your finger at someone else and try to pass the blame! Look, you priests, my complaint is with you! 5 As a sentence for your crimes, you will stumble in broad daylight, just as you might at night, and so will your false prophets. And I will destroy your mother, Israel. 6 My people are being destroyed because they don't know me. It is all your fault, you priests, for you yourselves refuse to know me. Now I refuse to recognize you as my priests. Since you have forgotten the laws of your God, I will forget to bless your children. 7 The more priests there are, the more they sin against me. They have exchanged the glory of God for the disgrace of idols." Hosea 4:1-7 (NLT)

Consequences eventually meet accountability. This is undoubtedly true in a religious sense, but not necessarily so in today's society. This is the reason so many people commit crimes again and again because there are no serious or immediate consequences. Juveniles are a prime example. They literally get away with murder because they know nothing will happen to them. If this isn't an example of lawless behavior, then I don't know what is. Juveniles eventually meet consequences either when they turn 18 years old, or when they meet the cold hand of death. They either spend time in jail because they are adults now, or they die before they reach 18. Consequences are all about making the right decisions. If we choose to do the things that God wants us to do then our accountability before Him will result in favorable consequences. When God is happy, everyone is happy. Why is that such a hard concept to grasp?

The absence of accountability and consequences may be the result of a lack of discipline. Its definition is: Training that develops self-control, punishment, set or system of rules and regulations. With this definition it is plain to see that discipline plays right in line with accountability and consequences. If one does not have the proper training or chooses to ignore it then there is no self-control or punishment. What kind of life would it be without any accountability of our self-control and penalties for actions? The absence of discipline suggests the presence of lawlessness and chaos. I think Katherine Hepburn points this out when she said, "Without discipline, there's no life at all." There is an undeniable relationship between discipline, accountability, and consequences. I will also go so far as to say that the lack of discipline breed's laziness. If you really stop and think about it, laziness itself is selfish behavior and demonstrates the lack of discipline and responsibility.

It took me quite a long time to realize this correlation even though I have heard my parents tell me a billion times that what goes around comes around. This is such a simple way of stating things. Without discipline, what comes back around is usually unpleasant. This happens because we are accountable for our actions, which also have consequences. See how all of these work together? I have shown these in a negative light so now I would like to bring out the positive aspect of discipline. Once again I will use one of my favorite examples in history to demonstrate my point. General Patton was a master of discipline towards his troops during World War II and was regimented about the training his troops received. This naturally established accountability in the direction of his command. His troops absolutely realized every consequence for violating any of the training rules or regulations. With this very strict discipline and accountability, his troops were willing to die in battle without any hesitation or question of any decision or order given to them by General Patton. He knew that with this kind of training, they were prepared to handle any situation. This is why he said, "A man who is aware of danger automatically takes steps to provide against it." Training and self-control can provide a way for positive consequences. We could make a list all day long of names that have proven this point. Here are just a few: Wilma Rudolph, Muhammad Ali, Abraham Lincoln, Bill Gates, Sir Winston Churchill, Elvis Presley, and George Washington. These people demonstrated an enormous amount of discipline to achieve success. As a matter of fact, Winston Churchill confirmed this when he said; "Success is the ability to go from one failure to another with no loss of enthusiasm." Now that is discipline. We can obviously use discipline to achieve positive goals and dreams. God promises us a reward if we have enough discipline to run the race and fight the good fight. Discipline is a must.

Let's not forget that when discipline is challenged or questioned for the sake of disagreement or ideology, then revolt and defiance can occur. Let's look at an example of Fascism. Here is what John Weiss points out about this issue: "And this is my major point; The radical right thrives in societies where older but still powerful conservative classes are threatened by rapid and modernizing social change; change which creates or gives strength to liberal and radical classes and groups antagonistic toward "the old ways." Discord and strife follow when people fail to use self-control and respect towards each other. They keep taking things to such extreme right and left that the distance is too great to ever compromise. These bring about all kinds of social and economic schisms.

Today in our society we have a definite lack of discipline with our youth. This has lead to defiance and decay of our nation. This is the breeding ground for gangs, Fascism, Nazis, Militias, and all kinds of drug problems. Our youth needs discipline, guidance and accountability. The million-dollar question of course is how do we accomplish this? If I had an answer for this question I would be a millionaire and be a guest on Oprah. All I know to do is stick to what God has instructed us through His word and be lead by His Spirit. I Thessalonians 5:19-22 (NLT) 19 Do not stifle the Holy Spirit. 20 Do not scoff at prophecies, 21 but test everything that is said. Hold on to what is good. 22 Keep away from every kind of evil.

The only thing I have to offer is what worked for my grandfather, my father, and myself. Maybe we need to acquaint today's youth with this drug problem. I had a drug problem when I was young. I was drug to church on Sunday mornings. I was drug to church for weddings and funerals. I was drug to family reunions no matter the weather. I was drug to the bus stop to go to school every weekday. I was drug by my ears when I was disrespectful to adults and teachers. I was also drug to the woodshed when I disobeyed my parents. Those drugs are still in my veins; and they affect my behavior in everything I do, say, and think. They are stronger than cocaine, crack, or heroin, and if today's children had this kind of drug problem, America might be a better place. We would know what the words accountability, consequences, and discipline mean. We would once again be people of character where your word is as good as gold. America needs to stand up and take responsibility for our society and its actions.

CHAPTER 3
RELIGION

"The foundations of our society and our government rest so much on the teachings of the Bible that it would be difficult to support them if faith in these teachings would cease to be practically universal in our country." President Calvin Coolidge

Captain Arduous was sitting in his chambers while scheming his next raid. One of his recently acquired crewmembers entered and asked him a question. During this conversation about what happens when people die he asked the Captain if he believed in God. He stopped his planning and sternly peered at his subject. "Do you think a god could give me plenty of gold, ships, women, rum, and everything I could ever want?" he asked. "I don't believe in any god. I am the supreme ruler of the seas. I take what I want when I want it. I have enough gold to buy any country, fleet, or crew. I believe that I can go anywhere and do anything. I guess that makes me a god. I suppose that I really do believe in god, me! " he exclaimed. With that statement the subject turned and left his chambers feeling outraged yet saddened. His religious upbringing foretold of certain self-destruction as a result of this kind of thinking, yet could he be bold enough to tell the Captain that he was on a collision course with certain doom? The final battle between Captain Arduous who claims to be god, and the one true God is inevitable.

Please relax because I am not going to say that a certain religion is right or wrong. That is not the intent of this chapter, nor of this book. It would be awfully hypocritical of me to show disrespect and be irresponsible by appointing myself as a religious judge. This would not only violate God's policy, but would ironically go against everything I have stated and stand for in this book. With this in mind, I would like to give my own definition of religion without proclaiming or offending any specific religion. Here is my definition. A belief and reverence in a Supreme being regarded as Creator of everything. A personal system grounded in such belief and worship. A set of beliefs, values, and practices based on the teachings of this Supreme being or Creator. A cause, principle, or activity pursued with zeal and conscientious devotion.

When I use the term religion I am not talking about a specific religion. I am talking about basic fundamental truths that most religions teach. I mean that no matter which church you are affiliated with, it should have taught you certain morals, ethics, and values. These things usually hold true no matter what race, gender, or age you are. Good morals, ethics, and values can traverse racial and cultural boundaries. Jesus was successful in teaching because he used basic truths that would cross socio- economic levels too. He used the same principles on both the rich and the poor. This is to say that God's word is truth. This truth is known around the world. Here is an example: "Thou shall not steal." (Exodus 20:15) Most countries will recognize and honor this age-old philosophy. This is to say that a universal code of religious ethics may be acknowledged and practiced. The key words regarding religion that I would like to explain in further detail are morals, ethics, and values. They are relatively close together in meaning and purpose. This is why I want to break them down individually to reveal each of their unique aspects. Then I will show how they compliment and support each other. This is the same manner a coach would view a team. A list of each individual players abilities would be studied so that an idea of how they can be incorporated as team in a more effective method may be implemented. This is a logical way of looking at content.

My whole point here is that Raiders have struck at the very core of our existence. They have wounded our religious teachings and philosophies for the sake individualism and humanism. They refuse to recognize the fact that religion is the foundation upon which we have established our existence. It is the common bond, which holds us together as one nation under God. That is why we should stand up and be proud that we have the right and privilege to say, "In God we trust." Raiders have fought long and hard to suppress the teachings and ideas of religious morals, ethics, and values in any public facility. If they succeed then our self- destruction is not far behind. This is not only a natural cycle of history, but also a promise from God. If we don't get rid of the venom the Raiders have smitten us with, then our fate will be the same as the Roman Empire. God usually sends warning signs reminding us to shape up and return to his ways or something very bad will happen. I feel we need to return to religious morals, ethics, and values in our lives in order to appease God's wrath. Society would be a much nicer place to live in if we all would adopt these religious principles. The benefits would be far greater than we can imagine. Wouldn't it be wonderful to try and find out? I hear many older people tell stories about how they never locked their houses or cars because everyone was respectful of each other's property.

I will first break down the word morals. Webster's defines it: honest, standing on convictions (integrity). The word integrity is in parenthesis because I will deal with it later in this section. I wanted to mention it right away for the significant light it sheds on the concept of morals. The whole idea behind integrity is firmness of character and being honest. It naturally blends with morals. Honesty has to be the base upon which these others will be built. Raiders have once again used their cut-throat techniques to try and rid their world of honesty. Proof is when you ask a Raider whom they can trust and they say, "No one". None of them are honest. It seems to me that our society has departed from the old saying, "Honesty is the best policy". We are filled with half-truths and little white lies. We keep fooling ourselves by trying to rationalize the idea that if nobody gets hurt, then a lie isn't bad. In order to practice healthy and positive morals, we must be honest with teachers, parents, others, and ourselves.

Our society has been infected by moral relativity through the tactics of Raiders. As I have been warning about over and over again, this infection can be fatal. Moral relativity believes that whatever I feel at the moment is right and acceptable, and therefore morally O.K. This can be situational and change like the weather depending on how I feel about whatever suits me. Other people's lives and feelings are of no importance or consequence to me. This has gone to such an illogical extreme. People actually can think it is O.K. to do something, but not when someone else does the same thing. For example, it is alright if I cheat on my spouse because that is what guys do, but it is not alright for her to cheat on me. Moral relativity is selfish and irresponsible.

Needless to say, that moral relativity is very dangerous, illogical, and immoral. Where is the honesty when you only care about yourself with a blatant disregard for others? Integrity has no part in moral relativity, and neither does God. Working as a police officer for several years has given me some exposure to the moral decay of society. A large percentage of problems are a result of alcohol and drug abuse. Raiders love to use them to cause severe damage and devastation to innocent lives. God best states the morality of alcohol in the book of Proverbs 20:1 (NKJV) "Wine *is* a mocker, Strong drink *is* a brawler, And whoever is led astray by it is not wise." The concept is that when we lower our standards of morality, it is easy for Raiders to take advantage of the situation. If we decide to take alcohol or drugs, it is not a wise and moral choice because it can quickly result in unpleasant consequences.

The whole point of morality is being honest and truthful. God is honest, truthful, loving, and the best example of integrity. Our morality should be based on His love and integrity. This is no big secret, nor is it something new. Jesus points this out when he says to love God with all of our heart, mind, soul, and strength. He then says to love our neighbor as ourselves. If we would stand on these convictions, then moral relativity couldn't exist. To me integrity is standing on what you know is morally right according to God's instructions. He gave everything He had to us because of His love for us. He keeps His promises. His morality, honesty, and integrity were as bright as the sun when he allowed Jesus to die for us. When was the last time we have seen someone behave with this kind of integrity and morality based on love?

Raiders have gained too many followers. I can't help but wonder if God inspired Sir Winston Churchill when he made the statement, "Never give in, never, never, never, never, in nothing great or small, large or petty, never give in except to convictions of honor and good sense. Never yield to force; never yield to the apparently overwhelming might of the enemy." This should be the motto for us when we stand against the enemy of Satan and his Raiders. We need to take a stand.

Here is what Raiders want us to forget. As you walk up the steps to the Capitol Building which houses the Supreme Court you can see near the top of the building a row of the world's law givers and each one is facing one in the middle who is facing forward with a full frontal view - it is Moses and the Ten Commandments! As you enter the Supreme Court courtroom, the two huge oak doors have the Ten Commandments engraved on each lower portion of each door. As you sit inside the courtroom, you can see the wall, right above where the Supreme Court judges sit, a display of the Ten Commandments! There are Bible verses etched in stone all over the Federal Buildings and Monuments in Washington, D.C. You would think that these Supreme Court Justices would constantly be reminded of them when they are making decisions for the benefit of our great nation. Sometimes I wonder if they take them for granted.

James Madison, the fourth president, known as "The Father of Our Constitution" made the following statement, "We have staked the whole of all our political institutions upon the capacity of mankind for self-government, upon the capacity of each and all of us to govern ourselves, to control ourselves, to sustain ourselves according to the Ten Commandments of God." Patrick Henry, that patriot and Founding Father of our country said, "It cannot be emphasized too strongly or too often that this great nation was founded not by religionists but by Christians, not on religions but on the Gospel of Jesus Christ". Every session of Congress begins with a prayer by a paid preacher, whose salary has been paid by the taxpayer since 1777. Fifty-two of the 55 founders of the Constitution were members of the established orthodox churches in the colonies. Thomas Jefferson worried that the Courts would overstep their authority and instead of interpreting the law would begin making law....an oligarchy....the government of few over many. The very first Supreme Court Justice, John Jay, said,

"Americans should select and prefer Christians as their rulers." How, then, have we gotten to the point that everything we have done for 220 years in this country is now suddenly wrong and unconstitutional? Raiders have enslaved us with moral relativity. When choosing a Supreme Court Justice, Christianity should be the very first prerequisite as to ensure proper morals, ethics, and values.

The second word relating to religion is ethics. Webster's defines ethics as: personal standards of right and wrong actions. If our personal standards are the same as God has established, then our actions should be righteous by His nature. It is important to choose behavior that is morally and ethically sound. This thought is brought out by the famous author Mark Twain when he states, "Each man must for himself alone decide what is right and wrong, which course is patriotic and which isn't. You cannot shirk this and be a man. To decide against your conviction is to be an unqualified and excusable traitor, both to yourself and to your country, let me label you as they may." I couldn't agree more with his statement. What a wonderful example from such a talented author. Sometimes I wish I had his talent to express my ideas and subject matter.

Raiders have slaughtered our sense of ethical behavior. There no longer exists any wrong actions, only what is right for me. This seems to be one of the favorite means to an end for Raiders. Our educational system is packed with this kind of sentiment and is filling our children with the same kind of non-ethical beliefs. For the past 6 years I have taught over 4,200 kids what it means to take a stand against drugs and violence and to make proper choices based on respect and responsibility. The sad part is seeing a number of these kids acting with no concept of what unacceptable behavior is. To them wrong is right. Some kids honestly believe that if they steal something from a store and don't get caught, then it makes it O.K. Somehow that wrong behavior suddenly becomes right. I remember breaking up a fight between two eighth grade boys because one of them said something bad about a girl in the hallway. Billy jumped Bobby because he overheard the comment Bobby had made about the girl. I asked Billy why he thought it was right to jump Bobby. He said because a girl shouldn't fight so he fought for her. I told him I understood where he was coming from, but it still did not make his actions justifiable. Billy still to this day believes he did nothing wrong in jumping Bobby. To him wrong was right. This is the philosophy of a Raider. Reasoning and logic somehow does not compute with Raiders.

I did come across a valuable resource to help combat against our kids lack of ethical education. I found a book called, "The Moral of the Story" by Bobby & Sherry Norfolk. They have incorporated morals and ethics through storytelling and fables. I recommend this book for those of you who want to be more effective in teaching children. Here is a statement from their book about teaching kids ethics in an effective manner: "To engage in the lessons of human character and ethics contained in our history and literature without resorting to empty preaching and crude didacticism is the great skill of teaching." — **Kevin Ryan** (Director of the Center for the Advancement of Ethics and Character) Boston University. Whatever method proves to be effective in our children's lives should be grafted with human character and ethical behavior.

Without the knowledge of which behavior is right or wrong, our society is in for a quick downfall. It is not hard to see that our society is declining in the same fashion as the Roman Empire. Raiders are tearing apart our ethics, morals, and traditions. This is obvious by the disappearance of politeness and manners, which by themselves, should coincide with our ethical beliefs. When you have courtesy and morality then you can have public order and decency. Edward Gibbon supports this idea through his work entitled "The history of the fall and decline of the Roman Empire". He reveals how the decline of the Roman Empire was paralleled by a decline in the morality of its citizens. I have previously mentioned the natural cycle of events concerning the Jews in ancient biblical times. This same cycle holds true for us today. God warns us about losing our ethics, morals, and religious convictions. He says in Obadiah 1:15 "The day is near when I, the Lord, will judge the godless nations! As you have done to Israel, so it will be done to you. All of your evil deeds will fall back on your own heads". No matter what civilization you choose as an example, the basic underlying principles are the same.

You will see the same kind of results for Captain Arduous and the world he thinks he controls. Even thought Captain Arduous is a fictitious character, the morals and principles from his escapades hold true for us as well. I made his character and actions to portray the same pattern as other civilizations that have not listened to wisdom or reason and have let self-gratification become their leader and eventually their demise.

To make all of this plain and in simple English, if a society permits each individual to decide what is right and wrong, then chaos and disorder will be the result. This will happen because there is no set standard of ethics. Each person will argue that their way is the best and this will result in disagreements, fights, injuries, and it only continues to get worse. When individuals become their own god, then the question of which god has the ultimate authority comes into play. When they try to settle this matter is when people get hurt either emotionally or physically. This is definitely not the kind of behavior that is designed and spelled out by the

Almighty God in His word. This is plain to see in AMOS 5:14-15 "Do what is good and run from evil-that you may live! Then the Lord God Almighty will truly be your helper, just as you have claimed he is. Hate evil and love what is good; remodel your courts into true halls of justice. Perhaps even yet the Lord God Almighty will have mercy on his people who remain." Let us decide what is right according to the instructions, which God has given to us so that we may live in peace and prosperity.

The last part of religion to be discussed is values. Once again, it is closely linked to morals and ethics, yet takes on it's own meaning and purpose. My definition is: basic principles, fundamental truths. You can already see how values blend right in with morals and ethics. Let me try to put all of these in perspective. A society that seeks out the truth of what is right or wrong (ethics) should take a stand upon these convictions once they are discovered (morals) because they should be based on God's principles (values). A promise of prosperity follows once everything is set in motion. Throughout history God has said he would send healing, harvest, good fortune, prosperity, and honest relations between each other if we would only apply His instructions to our lives. I know it is really hard to image what I am about to say, but think about it for a while and see if you can picture in your mind this concept. If our society truly based itself upon the morals, ethics, and values, which are handed down from the Almighty God in heaven, then we would have no need for the police, jails, courts, lawyers, judges, lie detectors, and everything else that we have for dishonest behaviors. All of these things exist for those who choose to do what is wrong. It is very hard to imagine an honest, God-fearing based society because we are so far removed from good values. Our country was supposedly formed with the same concept of healthy values, which I have just presented. A new nation, free to serve God and each other with honesty and respect was the idea our founding fathers had in mind. Somehow a bunch of Raiders have managed to spoil this simplistic and effective model. God has repeated the message to return to His ways several times from the beginning of time. Each time He warns of serious consequences if His counsel is not performed. Each time He has kept His promise.

Serving as a D.A.R.E. officer for over 6 years now, I have had the opportunity to help kids in several different ways. I have linked together with school counselors, pastors, youth directors, and various community leaders to provide assistance for any child who needs it. I feel a great sense of accomplishment when all of us work together for the benefit of a child and their family. Serving and meeting needs is what life is about.

I do have another thought to impart. If the idea of a society based on God's principles with no need for police, jails, courts, etc., threw you for a curve, then my next concept will send you into left field. If our religious organizations were truly functioning like God has intended His church to perform for our communities, then we would have no need for things like: special needs organizations, homeless shelters, rehab centers, retirement homes, orphanages, or any social organization promoting community service and brotherhood. Let me explain further before you throw this book across the room. I am NOT saying that service organizations are bad or not needed today in our society. Please know that I am NOT saying that our religious organizations are bad either. Both of them do a lot of wonderful things for people that deserve more recognition than what they receive. I am very glad that each of them provides services for our communities. To prove this point, I will say that I regularly attend church worship and community outreach efforts associated with this church, and

I also belong to a community service organization. If I thought either one was bad or not needed in our society today; then I obviously would not be a part of them. Since I am a part of them, then I can honestly say that they are the most effective means for me to serve the community. Someone else may find other avenues or means to help in some way, shape, form, or fashion. I hope you are still reading instead of picking this book up off the floor from throwing it across the room, or using as wadding for a package.

Now that you know for certain that I am NOT against religions and community organizations because I belong to both of them, let me reiterate my original premise. I wish that all Christian based religions would communicate, pull all of their resources together, and start effectively serving our communities. Churches could provide the same services and brotherhood bonds towards society the same way as social organizations do. If this were the case, then there would be no need for social organizations because our churches would be fulfilling societies needs along with a close bond of brotherhood ties. If our churches would accept God's morals, ethics, and values and work together for the common good of mankind, then society would definitely prosper. We should all work together on the same principles and fundamental truths, which is my definition for values. The churches and their followers would meet the needs of the community if we practiced this. Widows and orphans would be taken care of by religious convictions and not by some government program. Christians should help take care of each other and their community.
Let's take God's morals, ethics, and values and make them work for our benefit just as He has promised from the beginning.

If you have made it this far in this book, then you will definitely want to see some suggestions, ideas, concepts, and other beliefs to help our society. As I have said before, it would be very hypocritical of me to just write about what we are doing wrong, things that lead to destruction, and unheeded warnings without offering some ways to make things better or improve situations. So, believe it or not, I will present these things in the next chapter.

CHAPTER 4
REALIZATION

Captain Arduous was informed that some of his crewmembers were going back to their old traditional beliefs and refused to do some of the things they were commanded. One of these crewmen walked the plank for being bold enough to say out loud that impending doom was coming because of the Captain's ways. To silence the problem quickly, he thought he would drop off all of those members claiming to believe in God at the next small-uninhabited island. A day before this destination a severe wind picked up from the East. The wind and the waves tossed the ship around like a rag doll. Most of the crewmembers were cast overboard or drowned. After a few hours the ship and the sea were at rest again. Only the ones believing in God survived. When they reached the island a promise was made that they would never forget how God had liberated them from the dreaded Captain Arduous and at the same time saved them from the raging sea. They now have the chance to start their own world that believes in God and will definitely teach their children the importance of listening to God's truth and standing on it no matter what situation may come their way.

On the surface, this may seem to be quite a fictitious story. If you take a closer look then it should sound awfully familiar. Our country's genesis was shaped and molded in a similar way. Our roots were established upon the promise that we would be thankful to God for our deliverance and never forget His precepts. A new nation founded upon a universal code of ethics handed down from God would be ideal for everyone. Part of this nation's success was because of our determination to trust God through adversities. He will deliver us to our destination if only we will let Him be the driver. When mankind decides to be his own driver, it eventually results in a wreck. There are several examples in the bible and throughout secular history that prove this point. I will name a few from the bible so you can benefit from their stories: Cain, Jonah, Aquilla & Priscilla, and St. Peter. Here are some more examples from secular history: Julius Caesar, King Henry VIII, Napoleon, Hitler, and Saddam Hussein. Just image what this world would have been like if one or more of these people would have followed God's ways instead of their own. What kind of nation would they have established? Would it have still existed today? Only God knows.

I mentioned before that it wouldn't be fair or ethical if I just mentioned all of the negative and destructive results for not following a divine plan without offering some sort of remedy or solution. The title of this chapter is realization; the meaning of which is, to understand correctly, to make real. It is important for us to understand the situation we are in, and do something about it to make our plan of action real. No armchair quarterbacking is allowed. If I didn't supply a way to help then I would just be a whiner and complainer about our situation. It is just like my father used to say, "If you not part of the solution, then you are a part of the problem". I also like the words of Dale Carnegie when he said, "Any fool can criticize, condemn, and complain – and most fools do". I feel God would be pretty perturbed with me if I didn't share His directions and suggestions. The last thing I want to do is make God angry because of my negligence. I would rather not feel his wrath towards me. With this in mind, let's get right to point.
Earlier in this book I pointed out a natural cycle of events that has been repeated throughout history. It was prosperity,

neglect, warnings, then either repentance or destruction. I feel that our country has enjoyed times of prosperity. We have started to forget about God and are trying to take Him out of everything (neglect). There have been several warnings and messages for us to return to His instructions. This puts us in the position of either repenting or facing God's punishment.

Here is another cycle of events for us to consider as being a part of a solution that is acceptable to God. Obviously the first step is to repent or feel regret for something which has occurred and to change ones sinful ways. Part of true repentance is trying not to repeat the offensive action. The next step is to react or to act in response to, move in a reverse direction, do right. Something must be done and not just talked about to death. Once actions are taken then hopefully there will be a revamping or to patch and reconstruct something again. Let me put these into words that even someone like me can understand. We must turn our direction around 180°; choose to do the moral and ethical action, and then work like crazy to accomplish it. This sounds like a relatively simple idea and it is. That is the beauty of it all. God promised that He would take care of the difficult situations if we would just do our part. Our part is simple: turn to Him and follow. If we mess up, then apologize and learn how not to repeat that action in the future. Even I can understand this simple philosophy. As the title of this book suggests, Raiders have also attacked these other three R's: repentance, reacting, and revamping. This prevents us from enjoying the prosperity which God grants to us.

For some reason the first step seams like a doozy to a lot of people. I guess that Raiders have conditioned society to be callous and insensitive. It is difficult to repent if you don't feel sorry or responsible for your actions, especially when the blame is placed on others.

Repentance calls for a true change of heart. This is most difficult when a heart is cold or hardened. We have a true challenge before us to call a nation to repentance when the acceptable behavior is to say, "It's not my fault" or "It wasn't me". It is not impossible when God gets involved. Pharaoh's heart was hardened until God used Moses to show His power and plan. When Pharaoh saw the power of God at work, he then let the children of Israel go free. To prove my previous point, however, Israel would never have gone free if they had not remembered God's laws and instructions. The same holds true for us today because God is the same yesterday, today, and tomorrow. If we return to Him, He will restore our land and heal our people. This is the way our country started, and this is the way I hope to see us continue. Let me point out several reasons that our nation needs to have a change of heart towards God starting from the U.S. Supreme Court all the way down to the everyday person like myself. Here are some of the decisions we have made recently against God's instructions that we have accepted:

- Alabama Supreme Court ruling: Ten Commandments are unconstitutional and were ordered to be removed from the public square.
- San Francisco and Boston legalizes same sex marriage.
- Prayer in public schools is prohibited (9th district court ruling)
- California ruling to take the words "under God" out of the Pledge of Allegiance to the flag.
- US courts not holding Catholic priests accountable for child molestation and rape cases dating back several decades.

- Hollywood not accepting or recognizing Mel Gibson's movie about the Passion of Christ, criticism and false accusations about anti- Semitic messages.
- ACLU outraged by a picture of our US troops bowing their heads to pray while in the battlefield in Iraq.
- A federal judge ruled that Tennessee's "Choose Life" license plate is unconstitutional. U-S District Judge Todd Campbell said the plate "discriminates based on viewpoint" in violation of the 1st Amendment to the United States Constitution.
- Former President Clinton was impeached for lying under oath, yet still kept his office and position without consequences.
- The prohibition of The Fellowship of Christian Athletes to hold a prayer in the end zone before football games at public schools. `

It seems to reason that if you decide to be politically correct so you won't offend anyone or hurt some feelings, then you begin to take God out of society. I don't think I have ever discovered a passage from the bible where God has said it was O.K. to go against His instructions just so we won't be offensive. I don't think He told Noah to stop building an ark because it might be offensive, yet Noah and his family were the only survivors. The world had a chance to repent. Would Noah have finished the ark and listened to God if he would have listened to the people in order to be politically correct and not offensive?

I am not alone in feeling this way. Another prominent figure in our history was also very passionate about our religious obligation to our country. Patrick Henry once said, "It cannot be emphasized too strongly or too often that this great Nation was founded not by religionists, but by Christians; not on religions, but on the Gospel of Jesus Christ. For that reason alone, people of other faiths have been afforded freedom of worship here." This is who we are. If someone doesn't want to be a part of this, then they can either go somewhere else or be peaceful and respect what this country is all about. If you do not want to embrace Christianity and the principles it presents, then that is fine. You definitely have that right and can enjoy it. I feel, however, that it is a violation of most religion's ethics to be spiteful or hateful towards our fellow man and especially his religion based on God's laws and directions.

I just don't understand how any religion that claims to follow God can openly reject and defy another religion that is also following God. It just doesn't seem to fit the "love thy neighbor" concept. Here is my point. Yes, people have the Constitutional right to embrace any religion they choose. That right also includes stating opinions or disagreements about other religions. Does someone have the right to protest religious organizations and say all kinds of malicious propaganda? Yes! However, just because you can, doesn't mean you should. The more you take a stick and poke at a hornet's nest, the more likely you are to get stung. Someone can disagree with our country and its Christianity because they have that right here, but that doesn't mean they should buck the system, especially if they are not a citizen. If you do not like the fact that this country is based upon Christianity, that is fine, just don't go stirring things up and cause divisions. God absolutely hates someone that causes divisions, and so do I. That is the whole idea and meaning behind the phrase, "One nation, under God, indivisible, with liberty and justice for all." It is no wonder now that these were the concepts our nation was founded upon. Things

like, united we stand and divided we fall, and the inscription that is on our currency which is written in Latin, " E pluribus unum" should hold a sacred place in our heart. If we can't be united under God's direction and protection then we need to repent.
Our nation should repent and turn in the opposite direction to help and love each other rather than malign and fight against one another. It is a true Christian virtue to love one another, and pray for your enemies. It should be a true American attitude worth protecting and preserving for future generations to emulate.

I remember when there were six High School boys out one night after a party. They decided to get into a truck and play home run derby with over 26 mailboxes in the local area. Needless to say, they got caught. All of the boys and their parents agreed that "sorry" just wasn't going to cut it this time. The parents pulled together and decided to put the boys to work and fix every single mailbox that was damaged and go to the front door to apologize to every homeowner. Some of the boys really took this experience to heart and finally felt remorse for their actions. They felt they needed to do more to make up for their stupidity than just digging posts and fixing mailboxes. They decided to work at a car lot cleaning, sweeping, washing, taking trash out to the dump, and several other jobs to keep them busy. They put in about 200 hours of voluntary labor before their court date and without being told to do it. These boys truly repented. They felt bad for their actions and took the initiative to fix the damage they had caused. They moved in a reverse direction in order to do the right thing. If everyone had the attitude of these boys to learn from their mistakes and to correct problems, then we would be a much safer and secure society.

We can let go of foolish, selfish, pride in order to begin a life of healing and serenity the way that God has originally intended for us if we take the first step and truly repent.

When doctors have a patient that is in a coma, they wait for any kind of reaction from that patient to stimuli. In other words, they want to see the patient do or say something as a sign of improvement so they can help the patient further. The same concept applies now. God and I are waiting for our country to do or say something as a sign of improvement. We are waiting for our country to react with a true repentance. You will notice that the last part of the word react, is act. This is obviously a verb or command that denotes some sort of action or gesture. Something has to be done in order make things right again. I feel there are two kinds of reactions: natural, and planned. A natural reaction is one that is instinctive, use reflexes, or without a calculated thought process. Examples of natural reactions would be: eyes blinking when there is a lot of dust or dirt in the air, swatting at an insect flying around our face, reaching out to catch an infant about to fall, or swerving to miss hitting an animal in the roadway while driving. These actions happen quickly, without thinking, and feel like a natural action to take. This is why I have labeled them as natural reactions. The second kind is a planned reaction. This means you have used a thought process to look at different decisions and choices you would make in a given situation. In simple terms, you have a plan of action. You thought about what to do and plan to do it.

Sometimes natural reactions can be a result of training and repetition. This is what is known in the law enforcement community as "muscle memory." A police officer trains with a weapon so many times that the result is a natural reaction. They practice drawing and aiming until it becomes instinctive. The reaction is now automatically done without any hesitation from a step-by-step thought process. When a serious situation presents itself, a natural reaction of drawing a weapon and aiming occurs. It is possible to condition our minds and bodies to certain natural reactions. Sometimes we condition ourselves in a negative way. If someone reacts to people by being rude, obnoxious, vulgar, and disrespectful all the time, then they have conditioned themselves to react this way. Their natural reaction is now unpleasant to others.

We can train our minds and bodies to naturally react in either a constructive or destructive way. This is the concept behind anger management classes. The idea is to train your mind and body to have a positive natural reaction rather than one of anger, rage, and violence. This is why God wants us to be transformed by the renewing of our minds. He wants our natural reactions to be morally and ethically sound. This usually takes a lot of practice, discipline, and repetition until it finally becomes a natural reaction. It goes a little deeper than becoming a mere habit, it becomes an instinctive behavior. God gives instincts for protection, safety, and health. Man can decide to ignore God's design for instinctive behavior and pursue his own evil desires and lusts. This makes his instinctive behavior and judgments the same as a vicious animal with little or no control or regard for anyone else beside themselves. People who deliberately spread lies to try and persuade others to think the way they want them to are called false teachers. Their natural instincts are described in 2 Peter 2:12-19 (NLT).

(12) These false teachers are like unthinking animals, creatures of instinct, who are born to be caught and killed. They laugh at the terrifying powers they know so little about, and they will be destroyed along with them. (13) Their destruction is their reward for the harm they have done. They love to indulge in evil pleasures in broad daylight. They are a disgrace and stain among you. They

revel in deceitfulness while they feast with you.
(14) They commit adultery with their eyes, <u>and their
lust is never satisfied.</u> They make a game of luring
unstable people into sin. They train themselves to
be greedy; they are doomed and cursed. (17) These
people are as useless as dried up springs of water or
as clouds blown away by the wind – promising
much and delivering nothing. They are doomed to
blackest darkness. (18) They brag about themselves
with empty, foolish boasting. With lustful desire as
their bait, they lure back into sin those who have
just escaped from such wicked living. (19) They
promise freedom, but they themselves are slaves to
sin and corruption. For you are a slave to whatever
controls you.

It is plain to see the point I was making earlier when God's word is the basis of logic, understanding, and reasoning. God can guide our natural instinct if we let Him, or we can be guided by our own desires, that are doomed and cursed. We will be looking at the first part of this passage (2 Peter 2:1-12) in the next section when we explore the meaning of planned reactions. Right now I just want to make it clear that we do have natural reactions and the results of them depend on whether God or we ourselves are cultivating, directing, and maintaining them. Raiders are slaves to their own demise, for that is what controls them. This is what makes them so dangerous because they just don't care. Their method of madness does not have to rule over everyone. If we take a stand together for the cause of Christianity and righteous living, then we are promised a victory over such evil.

We need to spread the attitude of Jesus so that everyone will be kind to one another. This is plain to see in 2 Peter 1:3-9 (NLT).

"As we know Jesus better, His divine power gives us everything we need for living a godly life. He has called us to receive His own glory and goodness! And by that same mighty power has been given us all of His rich and wonderful promises. He has promised that you will escape the decadence all around you caused by evil desires and you will share in His divine nature. So make every effort to apply the benefits of these promises to your life. Then your faith will produce a life of **moral excellence**. A life of moral excellence leads to knowing God better. Knowing God leads to self-control. Self-control leads to patient endurance. And patient endurance leads to godliness. Godliness leads to love for other Christians. And finally you will grow to have genuine love for everyone. The more you grow like this the more you will become productive and useful in your knowledge of our Lord Jesus Christ. But those who fail to develop these virtues are blind or at least very shortsighted; they have already forgotten that God has cleansed them from their old life of sin."

God has promised us that if we try to apply His power in our lives, then He is faithful and will deliver us from evil and corrupt natural reactions through self-control and love. Our instincts will become righteous. Wouldn't that be a wonderful thing to see today?

The second kind of reaction is a planned one. This means you have a plan of action that you have considered. Elements include a motive, desire, instructions, and an opportunity. During this process there is a chance to review consequences of such actions and see the need to repent. Instead of doing so, the primal instinct takes over to produce ungodly actions. At any point in time we have the opportunity to change our evil plots and schemes plus use our energy and resources for the benefit of society. God already has a planned reaction for us when we choose to accept Him into our lives. Many different things are in store for us when we put God first. He is ready and willing to put His plan into action through our voluntary will. His promise is very clear in Ezekiel 11:17-21 (NIV),

> "Therefore say: I will gather you from the nations and bring you back from the countries where you have been scattered, and I will give you back the land of Israel again. (18) They will return to it and remove all its vile images and detestable idols. (19) I will give them an undivided heart and put a new spirit in them; I will remove from them their heart of stone and give them a heart of flesh. (20) Then they will follow my decrees and be careful to keep my laws. They will be my people, and I will be their God. (21) But as for those whose hearts are devoted to their vile images and detestable idols, I will bring down on their own heads what they have done, declares the Sovereign Lord."

If we repent from the idols in our lives, then God has promised to supply us with a pure heart and a new spirit. Idols are anything we apply to our lives that comes before God's instructions for us. This means that we can serve all kinds of idols when we allow them to come before our relationship we have with God. If God is not first, then the idol is. These idols may include: time, money, material things, other relationships, and even ourselves. That is right! We can make our own selves an idol. Our whole purpose as Christians is to let God take control of our lives so that our natural and planned reactions will not be evil, but guided by His righteousness and grace. I wish I could explain all the details about God's unlimited grace and love for us. This subject would be another book in the making. It is fascinating to me.

I am still in the learning process on these subjects so I will keep it on my level of understanding, which is kind of simple. If I apply my faith, He will use His power, and miracles will never cease. I am reminded of an old saying, "God said it, I believe it, and that settles it." This is stated in Hebrews 11:6 (NIV), "But without faith it is impossible to please God, because anyone that comes to him must believe that he exists and that he rewards those who earnestly seek him." True repentance means changing your heart and changing your mind. If we let our heart and mind work together through faith in God then we are promised a great reward. If you would like an explanation of how we can change our hearts and minds to let God work His will through us which is easy to read and understand, then I truly recommend a book by Juanita Bynum entitled, "Matters of the heart." She shows the importance of returning to God by using her life as a testimony. She also explains how society is perverse and doomed without the heart of God to direct it. She is affirming the same thing I have said about the damage from Raiders.

There is also victory and prosperity when God is respected. This same theme is further explained in 2 Peter 2:1-11,

> "There will be false teachers and prophets among us. They will cleverly teach their destructive heresies about God… Theirs will be a swift and terrible end. (2) Many will follow their evil teaching and shameful immorality. And because of them, Christ and his true way will be slandered. (3) In their greed they will make up clever lies to get hold of your money. But God condemned them long ago, and their destruction is on the way. (4) For God did not spare even the angels when they sinned; he threw them into hell, in chains of gloom,

and darkness until the judgment day. (5) And God did not spare the ancient world- except for Noah and his family of seven. Noah warned the world of God's righteous judgment. Then God destroyed the whole world of ungodly people with a vast flood. (6) Later, he turned the cities of Sodom and Gomorrah into heaps of ashes and swept them off the face of the earth. He made them an example of what will happen to ungodly people. (7) But at the same time, God rescued Lot out of Sodom because he was a good man who was sick of the immorality and wickedness around him. (8) Yes, he was a righteous man who was distressed by the wickedness he saw and heard day after day… (9) So you see, the Lord knows how to rescue people from their trials, even while punishing the wicked right up until the day of judgment. (10) He is especially hard on those who follow their own evil, lustful desires and who despise authority. These people are proud and arrogant, daring even to scoff at the glorious ones (angels) without so much as trembling. (11) But the angels, even though they are far greater in power and strength than these false teachers, <u>never speak out disrespectfully</u> against the glorious ones."

Let our planned reactions be to follow God's laws and He will heal our land. It is such a simple concept that people want to make it harder than it really is. God is bigger than any problem or crisis we can ever imagine or experience. Remember, He is the one that created everything in the universe with just His word. I think we should listen to His word.

CHAPTER 5
REFLECTION

Our society has started a downward spiral towards its own demise by letting respect, responsibility, and religion deteriorate. These are what our nation was supposed to be founded upon, and now we are breaking up that foundation. How can we expect our nation to continue standing without a solid foundation? In order for us to continue as one nation under God, we must turn back to Him. Our second goal must be to take everything we have learned and try not to make the same mistakes again. This reminds me of the definition of insanity, which is, trying the same thing the same way and expecting a different result. If we keep going back to our sinful ways and expect God to bail us out then we must be insane. This is why repentance is a complete turn around process. You don't go backwards to where you came from, you go forwards towards God's direction. I mentioned several people in an earlier chapter to be examples of what happens when we refuse to turn around towards God.

I will now reveal some similarities with the decline and fall of the Roman Empire. The same principals hold true as mentioned in the first four chapters. Rome was a great civilization. It enjoyed times of prosperity. Rome definitely acquired a lack of respect for its authority figures. Senators and leaders became increasingly corrupt which caused a lack of trust and respect for their leadership. They were neglecting their responsibility to the people and also to each other. They became just like the pirates in the opening of each chapter in this book. Religious beliefs became so adulterated to the point where any belief was accepted and practiced regardless of its influence on society. Anything became a god to them, and they decided to enjoy it that way. They became selfish, destructive, and immoral. These negative characteristics were their religious beliefs. Good, proper, sound, and healthy morals, ethics, and values were ignored and therefore not taught to the next generation. The downward spiral continued to get worse. God started taking a back seat to society because people thought they could do things without his help and guidance. Several warnings were given to return back to the one true God. Rome refused to repent, and experienced a devastating downfall. I am presenting this example because it is so much like our society today that it is scary. One reason for pointing out these similarities is because I don't want people to be ignorant of history. Those ignorant of history are doomed to repeat it. I do not want a repeat. Let me now begin by paralleling our societies mistakes that are leading us toward a downfall, just like ancient Rome's decline and fall.

Our society is discarding traditional morality, a condition immediately marked by the disappearance of manners, which are dictated by morality. Politeness is a prerequisite for public order, which is why the improving and understanding of a waxing community constantly refine it. Edward Gibbon documents the opposite result in his work "The history of the fall and decline of the Roman Empire.", which reveals that the decline of the Roman Empire was paralleled by a decline in the morality of its citizens. **Philip Atkinson** (October, 1999)

The author here makes some very good points, which support my ideas, statements, and experience. The above paragraph accurately condenses the whole concept and philosophy of this book. When a democratic society starts abandoning the training and instruction in the social graces that help form a standard of moral traditions, then the generations growing up without them start becoming defiant, selfish, and egocentric. They become parents who fail to teach the moral traditions of the previous generation and the result is a society of offspring continuing the generative cycle towards a decline in the moral and social structure of society.

I discovered a list of moral traditions that were called etiquette. Living close to Vanderbilt University gave me the opportunity to explore the social graces once used by the Vanderbilt family. Let me share a list from Amy Vanderbilt's complete book of etiquette (1958). While exploring this list, make a mental note of how many our society has abandoned today, and are not being taught by parents. I feel the results you discover will be a little apocalyptic. Here is what she said from pages 512-513 under polite society behavior for children:

George Washington is said to have lived by 54 maxims on personal conduct that cover actions and attitudes found to be socially acceptable and polite… I believe a child should eventually come to understand that publicly in "polite society" we **do not** do the following things:

- Scratch, pick teeth, spit, comb hair, or tend to nails.
- Chew with our mouths open or with obvious noise or lip-smacking.
- Leave a spoon in a cup or eat with a knife.
- Tuck in a napkin, or suck our fingers instead of wiping them on a napkin.
- Sit down to a meal unwashed, uncombed, or improperly dressed.

- Fail to greet others encountered in the household when we arise and when we return home.
- Tilt chairs or push them back from the table with all our body weight upon them.
- Lounge on the dinner table or put our elbows on it except between courses or sit on our spines.
- Go up and down stairs like elephants and bang doors after us.
- Pass in front of others without saying, "Please excuse me" or "I'm sorry".
- Use a flat "No" or "Yes" in answer to questions instead of "Yes Ma'am or Yes Sir".
- Speak ill of the dead or repeat damaging gossip.
- Swear in a way that is generally considered offensive.
- Put more than a manageable mouthful in our mouths at one time. Burp, belch, sneeze, or cough without attempting to turn away from others and then only behind the cupped hand or a clean handkerchief.

I have never seen a child with well-mannered parents who grew into an adult completely devoid of social grace. But I have seen such a child, in rebellion at constant goading concerning his manners, go through a savage period during which the only conformity with social customs was enforced with damaging tension to both child and parents.

How much of ourselves did we see in that list? If you sit on a park bench or at a booth in a fast food place, how many of these do you think you could pick out that people are doing

77

or not doing? Take a look at the younger generation and observe their behaviors. Now take a look at their parents and see if they are a mirror or reflection of their parent's behavior. George Washington put into place this code of conduct because he realized it was based on Christian morals, ethics, and values. It shouldn't seem odd to us today that polite manners are part of righteous Christian behavior. The success of George Washington is without a doubt in direct proportion to his foundation in Christianity. This not only guided him in his life, but in his presidency as well. He realized the importance of Christianity on a personal level and on a social level. These would in turn form a country based on God's behavioral guidelines. Since God is peace and love, and we base our society on Him, then our society should be full of peace and love. When we stop depending on God, we turn towards chaos and hate. George Washington started a Christian based country, but it is up to us to teach our children the importance of this first principle. If we neglect our responsibility of training our children in the ways of Christian morality, then we set into motion a society of self-destruction. Take a look around and see the evil things kids are doing as a lack of training and knowledge. If they are not trained in Christian morality, then they train themselves in destructive, humanistic behavior.

I have another list I would like to point out. The previous one was to take a look at manners, which children do or do not display in relation to whether or not they have been taught Christian morals. Christian morals, ethics, and values are a result of communal practice, and are the lexis of social wisdom. Now we are going to see a list of behaviors and discover their relationship to Christian morality on a societal level. Take a look how our country started out, where it is today, and where it's going in the future. This all depends on if we start going back to God's instructions for Christian living. Let's see how much has changed without Christianity since the end of World War II. Philip Atkinson has comprised this list and I will add a few bits and pieces to it. My comments will be in parenthesis at the end. Since 1950 our society has abandoned the following:

- Murderers are executed. (Inmates with several death sentences have been kept alive for over 10-30 years)
- Suicide is a crime with failed suicides liable to be punished by the law.
- Justice must be seen, the names of criminals and their accusers are <u>no longer published</u>.
- Men are expected to strive to behave like gentlemen, women like ladies. (Each gender should act like it's proper gender)
- Ladies before gentlemen - a direction for males to always give way before females thereby ruling who should go through a door first etc (Thank the feministic movement for the extinction of this courtesy)
- A gentleman always gives up his seat for a lady who is standing
- Children should only speak to adults when spoken to by adults. (Unfortunately this is a very rare occurrence)
- Children should be seen and not heard by adults. (Kids being quiet in public places like libraries, churches, post offices, super markets, etc.)
- Children are chastised at the discretion of an adult if they are insolent. (Children being spanked for back talking, sassing, and disrespect)
- Children are expected to surrender their seat so an adult can sit down.

- Unless people involved know each other intimately they should address each other by their title and surname – Mrs. Smith, Master Brown, Miss Adams. Titles have disappeared along with the use of surnames.
- Strangers must address each other as Sir or Madam.
- People in authority are addressed as Sir or Madam. (Police officers being respected and called Sir)
- School children refer to each other by surname. (Birth names being used instead of insignificant nicknames)
- Matters between family members are domestic disputes and are not the concern of the law. (Violence never being used in family disputes)
- The father is the head of the household, and his word is law. (Fathers being responsible towards their children and spouse)
- A father is expected to be the sole breadwinner for the family. (Fathers making proper financial decisions to support a family)
- A mother is expected to devote her time to her family and her home. (Feminists and females not being offended by this)
- Housework is the responsibility of the female members of the family, and is not a concern for the adult males. (Males being the handyman and working hard to fix everything for the family)
- Meals are prepared by the mother for the whole family to sit down and dine together. (Families dining together)
- Each family has a doctor who has long experience of the family and visits when his

patient feels too ill to attend surgery. (Knowing your doctor)
- A family consists of two heterosexual parents and children. (This being the majority and accepted norm in society)
- A family with only one child is considered to be raising a spoilt child.
- Childless parents are pitied as being unable to achieve pregnancy.
- The social stigma of divorce which is considered a sign of failure. (Divorce being seen in a negative light rather than acceptance)
- Marriage is permanent unless one partner dies, or betrays the other sufficiently for divorce; which is then resolved by a trial which identifies and punishes the guilty partner. (AMEN! Marriage being taken seriously)
- Wives promise to <u>obey husbands</u> as part of their marriage vows. (Husbands respecting their wives and keeping their vows too)
- Couples who live together out of wedlock are considered to be *living in sin*, and receive no legal recognition of their status. (This being taught as deviant behavior and not acceptable)
- Only a virgin bride is entitled to wear a white bridal gown. (Virginity being taught and still existing)
- If an unmarried man makes a girl pregnant he is expected to marry the girl. (Males taking responsibility for this action)
- A child born out of wed-lock is a bastard and despised as a product of sin. With the cost of raising the child to be born by the identified father or the mother. (Males being physically,

socially, and economically responsible for any child generated)
- The social stigma for being an unmarried mother; she receives no pension from the state and is despised as sinful. (No welfare or food stamps for unmarried mothers)
- A man and a woman can only share a hotel room if they are married
- Imperial Measure (<u>replaced by metric</u>)
- The <u>Hippocratic Oath</u> (Doctors doing no harm to patients)
- Smoking is a pleasurable activity which is only forbidden in areas where a flame is dangerous, or in those few areas set aside for non-smokers; the bottom deck of double-decker buses, the odd railway carriage. (Smoking being offensive in public to non-smokers and a health risk)
- Christian names have a standard spelling, see those displayed by the girls on store check-out. (Christian names meaning something)
- Neighbors are expected to be quiet. (Knowing your neighbors)
- Work attire is expected to be smart unless the demands of the job make it impossible. (Proper and modest work attire)
- Men are expected to wear a neck-tie at the office.
- Men have short hair, women have long hair. (Accepting one's gender)
- Only men are soldiers, police constables, boxers, footballers, bus drivers, etc. (No cases of sexual harassment)
- Homosexuality is an illegal and despised activity. (Deviant behavior)
- Nudity is forbidden in the media and in public areas. (Nudity is wrong)

- A public display of a mother breastfeeding is considered indecent.
- Swearing is forbidden in the media and public places. (Swearing and cursing being considered deviant behavior and wrong)
- Children are taught curb drill as soon as they attend school for their safety depends upon it. Traffic is not expected to slow down outside schools. (Showing respect for school zones and crossing guards)
- Customers are served by, and are expected to take the goods selected by, the shopkeeper. (Personal service)
- People are expected to go to church or Sunday school on the Sabbath. (Habitual attendance of a community church)
- Tradesmen are expected to use the rear door to announce their presence.
- Celebration of a life-times service to one firm upon retirement with presentation of a time-piece. (Loyalty to jobs and employers)
- Manners, Customs and Traditions are established by communal experience, and are the expressions of social wisdom. (Listening to the older more experienced and wiser people)
- The stigma of having a *dead-end* job. (Desire to achieve more)
- Celebration of Guy Fawkes on the evening of November 5th.
- Hair is dyed a natural color. (The color it's supposed to be)
- Labels appear on the inside rear of a garment. (Proudly being made in the U.S.A. labels on garments)

- Red Light means traffic must stop until a green light shows. As of 1999 it is possible to see drivers deliberately ignore red traffic lights; they do not just speed in an attempt to beat the red light, but halt at the red light, check the intersection, then proceed. (Being respectful of all traffic signs and courteous to other drivers)
- Infants are kept separate from adult work and play. Since the year 2000, I have witnessed infants being minded at work and adult dinner parties. Babies now (2003) accompany their mothers to parliament and high school. (Children being more important than careers)
- Headlines of newspapers are printed with a capital letter starting each word. Circa 2003 only the first word has a capital letter. (Using proper English rules and guidelines in the media)
- (Women reporters not being permitted in men's locker rooms)

I am sure we could compile a list that would be a book all its own. I did not say that I agreed with everything on this list by Phillip Atkinson, I just wanted you to see how traditions, manners, morals, ethics, values, and common courtesies have been abandoned. I am not saying that all of our founding traditions were good either. For example, I feel it was right and just to have abandoned the tradition of slavery. Once again I must emphasize that our behaviors must be acceptable to God in order to be Christian society. The importance of parents teaching children moral Christian behavior is vital to the essence of society. This is why Edward Gibbons says, "The inevitable scapegoat for people impatient of restraint must always be parents, because these are society's agents for teaching private restraint. So the cherished notions of the parents are always subject to attack by their maturing off-spring. This resentment of tradition was observed in his own civilization by Polybius (c. 200-118 BC), the Greek historian, who said: "For every democracy which has enjoyed property for a considerable period first develops through its nature an attitude of discontent towards the existing order." Children that are not being taught Christian values will eventually learn to resent and rebel against these older more traditional Christian values.

A clear example of this today is the attitude to be politically correct as not to offend anyone. Political correctness is a very humanistic and self-centered value that is being taught and accepted. It directly contradicts the concept of a majority rules democracy. It also violates God's instruction of loving your neighbor more than yourself. Being courteous, polite, and loving is the backbone of Christianity. If I proclaim to be a Christian and am trying to follow His ways, then I should not say anything offensive to anyone in the first place. If society is following the ways of Christianity, then there shouldn't be anything offensive said or done to anyone. Political correctness does not exist in this type of environment full of morals, ethics, and values based on Christianity.

When these simple traits are abandoned then selfish political correctness rises and heads towards a declination in society. I feel that political correctness is a humanistic attempt to replace the Christian value of being nice to people. It may also be the resentment of spoiled kids trying to get back at their parents because they were not properly taught Christian values. If people today would practice the principles of religious morals, then a godless and decaying society would not feel the need for political correctness. The whole purpose of political correctness is to stop offensive people from being offensive. If the offensive people were taught and practiced Christian principles, then they would learn not to be offensive anymore because it is not an acceptable behavior. That is why we need Christian values and not political correctness, because God's way is always the better one with positive results.

Let me try and summarize the whole concept and principle of this book. Our society, and those I call Raiders, are quickly leaving the sound and healthy Christian morals that helped start our great nation. The most important ones being: respect, responsibility, and religion. When they are not taught and passed down to the next generation, then these morals are replaced with whatever morals the next generation sees fit. The more this continues, the more society will decline and destroy itself. The great Roman Empire had its chance to embrace Christianity and its values. Rome decided to continue without God's direction. It had every opportunity to repent and revamp its existence. Rome continued declining and finally fell by destroying itself. Christianity did not, and still exists. Which example should we live by then, the one that is self-destructive, or the one from God that endures? Our great nation is following in the same direction and in the same manner that caused the demise of the Roman Empire. Shall we accept the same fate, or choose to repent and revamp our way of life to conform to real Christian values? The best summary is to listen to God and teach his instructions to our children. God has promised His blessings and prosperity if we only let Him guide us. I am including Deuteronomy 28:1-15 so you won't have to go look it up because it is so important. God clearly gives us His instructions and warnings. Will we listen?

DEUTERONOMY 28:1-15 (Basic English Version)

DE 28:1 Now if you give ear to the voice of the Lord your God, and keep with care all these orders which I have given you today, then the Lord your God will put you high over all the nations of the earth:

DE 28:2 And all these blessings will come on you and overtake you, if your ears are open to the voice of the Lord your God.
DE 28:3 A blessing will be on you in the town, and a blessing in the field.
DE 28:4 A blessing will be on the fruit of your body, and on the fruit of your land, on the fruit of your cattle, the increase of your herd, and the young of your flock.
DE 28:5 A blessing will be on your basket and on your bread-basin.
DE 28:6 A blessing will be on your coming in and on your going out.
DE 28:7 By the power of the Lord, those who take arms against you will be overcome before you: they will come out against you one way, and will go in flight from you seven ways.
DE 28:8 The Lord will send his blessing on your store-houses and on everything to which you put your hand: his blessing will be on you in the land which the Lord your God is giving you.
DE 28:9 The Lord will keep you as a people holy to himself, as he has said to you in his oath, if you keep the orders of the Lord your God and go on walking in his ways.
DE 28:10 And all the peoples of the earth will see that the name of the Lord is on you, and they will go in fear of you.
DE 28:11 And the Lord will make you fertile in every good thing, in the fruit of your body, and the fruit of your cattle, and the fruit of your fields, in the land which the Lord, by his oath to your fathers, said he would give you.
DE 28:12 Opening his store-house in heaven, the Lord will send rain on your land at the right time, blessing all the work of your hands: other nations will make use of your wealth, and you will have no need of theirs.
DE 28:13 The Lord will make you the head and not the tail; and you will ever have the highest place, if you give ear to

the orders of the Lord your God which I give you today, to keep and to do them;

DE 28:14 Not turning away from any of the orders which I give you today, to the right hand or to the left, or going after any other gods to give them worship.

DE 28:15 But if you do not give ear to the voice of the Lord your God, and take care to do all his orders and his laws which I give you today, then all these curses will come on you and overtake you:

The rest of the chapter in Deuteronomy lists all of the curses and bad things to come if God is not obeyed. I did not include them because we already know the end result. I wanted to include the only option and solution that will heal and restore our great nation. May we always choose the blessings from God and not His curses. I pray this book has inspired you to repent and revamp your life so that God can direct you. Change your life in order to receive God's blessings and prosperity so you may help someone else do the same. That is what Christianity is all about and our nation should reflect the same. This is my goal and prayer for my neighbors, my country, and myself. Let's not be Raiders of the lost R's.

God please forgive my heart and mind of selfish ways. Fill me with your Word and love so I may train others and myself in your ways. Let me stand for your Truth and Righteousness. Heal our hearts and our lands so they may become full of respect and honor for your sake. Thy Kingdom come, Thy will be done on earth as it is heaven. Amen.

A FATHER'S JOY

By: Steven Wright dedicated to Zachary Wright

I remember that amazing day when my life was filled with joy,
My cup of blessings overflowed, I was told I'm having a boy.
The emotions I felt when he was born are the best I ever had,
My dream had finally come true and I was suddenly a dad.

I could never really imagine how things would quite be
Fears and inhibitions melted when his face at last I could see.
I know God sent His angels to carry him to me from above,
And sweetly come to rest in his Father's arms full of love.

Every day I want to hold him for just another little while
Just so I can watch him laugh, play, and give me a smile.
The miracle of fatherhood comes to me now with no surprise

I experience God's love when we look in each other's eyes.

A Father's love for his son is an unexplainable pride,
Because absolute love from the Spirit dwells inside.
God grants us His love we think we can't understand
Until my son reached out and took hold of my hand.

I will always love and protect him for the rest of my days,
While trying to teach and guide him in the narrow way.
When my time comes, looking down from heaven I will be
A Father waiting to be with his son again so anxiously.

Thank you God for being my Father, and granting me the honor to make you proud of your son. I will give glory to the family name.

BIBLIOGRAPHY

Atkinson, Philip. "A Theory of Civilization" Oct. 2000 <http://www.ourcivilisation.com/index.htm>

Bartlett, John. Bartlett's Familiar Quotations. Canada: Little Brown & Co., 1992

Dobson, Dr. James. Bringing Up Boys. Wheaton, Illinois. Tyndale House Publishers Inc., 2001

Essame, Major General H. Patton A Study In Command. N.Y.: Scribner's Sons, 1974

Kidney, Walter C. Webster's 21st Century Dictionary. Nashville: Thomas Nelson Publishers, 1993

Nardo, Don. The Decline and Fall of the Roman Empire. San Diego: Lucent Books, 1998.

Norfolk, Bobby & Sherry. The Moral of The Story. Little Rock: August House, 1999

Vanderbilt, Amy. Amy Vanderbilt's Complete Book of Etiquette. Garden City, NY: Doubleday and Co., 1958

Weiss, John. The Fascist Tradition. NY: Harper and Row Publishers, 1967

General Observations on the Fall of the Roman Empire in the West
by Edward Gibbon

From the book Raising up boys, **Dr. James Dobson**
Robert D. Putnam Bowling Alone: The Collapse and Revival of American Community
Pages 100-101

Tyndale Charitable Trust. Holy Bible, New Living Translation. Wheaton, Illinois: Tyndale House Publishers, 1996

Value Soft. The Bible Collection Deluxe. (Basic English Version Bible) Waconia, MN. 2002.

www.ingramcontent.com/pod-product-compliance
Lightning Source LLC
Chambersburg PA
CBHW032021040426
42448CB00006B/692